A Personal Note from the Author,

RABBI MOSHE EISEMANN

Many years ago, I got involved in working to educate Jews from the Former Soviet Union through the Vaad Hatzolas Nidchei Yisroel. We discovered that in a residential day school, we could both educate and allow children to live as Jews full time. In 1990 Kishiniev Yeshiva was born.

We were given a building that used to be a synagogue. Before the Holocaust, the city of Kishiniev had 70 shuls, there were seforim published and there was even a Kishiniever Rebbe. Jews had been living there for centuries.

It's all gone now except for a few books, pictures and these few bright faces learning in our little Kishiniev Yeshiva.

It's a good school and I'm proud to be the "Rosh Yeshiva." As I write today in December, 2004, there are 40 boys and girls ages 12 –17 in two small but comfortable buildings. We know today of 80 graduates of the Kishiniev Yeshiva, both men and women who are living as proud and observant Jews. Some of them are married with children. Many are completing their education in the U.S. Some of them are teaching the next generation in the former Soviet Union. It's a small start and we would like to do more. However, it is costly work.

As a way of easing the burden, I came up with the idea of writing a series of simple, short books of Torah in the hopes that those who received them would help us. Many people have been generous, but the need continues.

I know there are many, many very important demands on you. I hope you will consider adding us to the list of the many projects you support. My address and phone number are listed below.

You can learn more about Kishiniev Yeshiva or donate online at *www.kishinievyeshiva.com*. On this site you can purchase many of my books. You can listen to or download tapes of classes I've given. We will be charging a modest fee for the books and the classes. We assure you, every penny you spend on our web site will benefit Kishiniev Yeshiva. Unlike a normal store, we will accept donations in excess of the "cost" of our products.

Rabbi Moshe Eisemann

Rabbi Moshe Eisemann

401 Yeshiva Lane, Apt 201
Baltimore, MD 21208
410-485-7396

OF PARENTS & PENGUINS

REFLECTIONS CONCERNING
THE EDUCATION OF
OUR CHILDREN
AND OURSELVES

MOSHE M. EISEMANN

FELDHEIM PUBLISHERS
JERUSALEM · NEW YORK

**Moshe M. Eisemann
401 Yeshiva Lane
Baltimore, MD 21208
(410) 484-7396
www.KishinievYeshiva.org**

Distributed by:
FELDHEIM PUBLISHERS
POB 35002, Jerusalem, Israel 91350
200 Airport Executive Park, Nanuet, N.Y. 10954
www.feldheim.com

Printed in the USA

ISBN 1-58330-184-4

10987654321

TABLE OF CONTENTS

WHAT IS THIS BOOK ALL ABOUT?
SOME REFLECTIONS ABOUT THE REFLECTIONS

OF PARENTS AND PENGUINS

ENDNOTES

WHAT IS THIS BOOK ALL ABOUT?

SOME REFLECTIONS ABOUT THE REFLECTIONS

EASY TARGETS

OF PARENTS AND PENGUINS. It is really a rather silly title; more eye-catching than substantive, more Madison Avenue hype than descriptive of a serious analysis of a very, very serious matter. So why use it?

I found myself asking this question as the book nears publication. What made me think, I wondered, that a catchy title would recommend my modest contribution more effectively than something more staid and proper like *Chinuch HaBanim*, or *Educating Our Children*? I am, after all, writing for a public composed of committed Jews, thoughtful people all, who want to do what is right, think what is right, read what is right, and to be serious about it. So why be flippant?

I decided to put my intuition to the test. I opened some newspapers and magazines lying around my home, publications which are directed to the very same readership which, I hope, will be interested in my little book. I scanned the advertisements and was shocked by the banal hyperbole which flew at me from every side. Jewish books were "lavishly illustrated", and "liberally sprinkled...."; Torah journals were "a great gift idea"; housing in Torah enclaves conformed to the "latest concepts", and the builders were famous for their "legendary commitment"; inspirational tapes dealt with "virtually every aspect of Jewish life"; and seminaries catered exclusively to a "select group" and to "outstanding graduates". And so on and on, and depressingly on. It took me just five minutes to come up with these few samples.

It seems that I am not far off the mark. The professionals must know what they are doing. They speak the language to which we listen. And like so many Pavlovian mutts, we salivate at the delicious goodies they throw our way.

Why have we become so shallow? Or to put it in a form which leads directly to the heart of a book which purports to deal with chinuch issues, where did our parents go wrong? Why did all the love and caring, and yes, very often profound wisdom with which they raised us, not produce people with more sense than we seem to evince? What element was there in our culture which frustrated their hopes for us, and will, unless we are willing to face some unpalatable truths, puncture our well-meaning efforts to make good and serious Jews of our children?

The answer, I believe, lies in the defining ethos of modernity, a way of perceiving and apprehending the world, which has relentlessly and, as we shall presently demonstrate, maliciously swept all before it since the beginning of the last century.

I quote from an essay by Dr. Moshe Sokol:

> According to Peter Berger, the sociologist of religion, "the theme of indi-

vidual autonomy is perhaps the most important theme in the world view of modernity." A product of Enlightenment thinking, the impact of individual autonomy can be felt in every sphere of contemporary life, from the political to the personal. Such ideas as individual rights, responsibility and freedom, and the importance of making one's own decisions and finding things out on one's own are all associated with the concept of autonomy.[1]

There, it seems to me, lies the enemy. It is the insistence upon the autonomy of the individual that has made a shambles of the *chinuch* which we received. Ideas and methods which were appropriate to other cultural milieus simply could not prosper when forced to deal with such an entirely new and potentially pernicious doctrine.

It all sounds innocuous enough and even resonates well with ideas that are congenial to us. There is indeed a great deal of dignity vested in the individual created in the image of God. Still, a careful reading should raise some questions. We are all for individual rights. Or are we? It seems that in Judaism there is precious little talk of rights and a great deal of stress on duties. "Individual rights and responsibilities" are fine but "freedom" is not without its ambiguities. The חירות which we celebrate on Pesach carries very different semantic freight than does "freedom" as it is understood in contemporary usage. Our ideal is to become servants [...ה' עבד משה] with as little freedom as possible [רשאי אינך אבל אתה יכול...תוכל לא]. The Torah itself leaves us in little doubt: *...For they are My servants whom I took out of Egypt that [I might] be Lord over them* [Vayikra 25:22][3].

And what, precisely, does "making one's own decisions" mean? And where, once we have defined it accurately, does it lead?[4] The idea, in its above form, and as explicated accurately by Dr. Sokol, was articulated from a secular viewpoint which has nothing at all to do with Judaism. We will not expect to find "Torah" there[5], and because of this it is of only limited use to us.

Let us then come back home and learn a little Gemara.

אמר רשע "אין רם" -- THE WICKED SAY, "THERE IS NOTHING WORTHY OF RESPECT!" [Bava Basra 78b]

The late Rav Hutner זצ"ל, Rosh HaYeshiva of Yeshivas Rabbeinu Chaim Berlin, was without a doubt one of the premier educators of our generation. He had his own way of doing things. His students were well aware that he expected to be treated with the absolute respect due to someone of his stellar accomplishments and high standing. Thus, after a meeting with him they

iv

would back out of the room making sure always to face him as they left. He was treated like royalty. That is what he demanded and that is what was done.

In his famous eulogy on Rav Hutner, Rav Shlomo Wolbe explained what lay behind this unusual insistence, one which in a lesser person might have been perceived as overbearing conceit.

Rav Hutner was determined that the young men under his care would not fall victim to the destructive "אֵין רם" of which the gemara speaks and which is so pervasive in our benighted times. The egalitarian *mishmash* which democracy run amuck has made of our society would not gain entry into the Bais HaMidrash of Yeshivas Rabbeinu Chaim Berlin. The orderly hierarchy, which is the basis of the Torah's organization of society,[6] would be maintained. Rebbi would be Rebbi and student would be student[7]. People would learn to submit and in submission find their own self respect.

When autonomy trumps, when אֵין רם is the slogan of the day and acts as the great equalizer, then the only arbiter of worth and value is the self. And the self, at the end of the day, can be a pretty sorry specimen. It is no great surprise that it gets the leadership which it deserves, the art which it deserves, the reporting and writing which it deserves, the politics which it deserves and the advertising which it deserves.

The educational enterprise, if it is to be worthy of that name, must realize what it is up against. It is a fine line that we must tread. We do not want to produce nonentities without minds of their own, but conversely, we do not want to produce fools who see only themselves as arbiters of right and wrong. It is not easy to maintain a posture which allows for a bowed back and a straight spine at one and the same time. It is possible, nevertheless.

OF SPINES AND SNAKES

Bava Kama 16a has this to say: "Seven years [after his death] man's spine turns into a serpent but only if he did not bow down during the *modim*[8] prayer."

What does this mean?

Maharal explains as follows: Among all the creatures on earth only man stands naturally erect. This most dignified and imposing of postures is a mark of royalty and is appropriate to man to whom the entire physical world is to be subservient. Tradition has it that originally the snake too was straight-backed. It had been designated as king of the animal world.[9]

But this distinction was taken away from the snake. The mark of true leadership is the ability to submit to ["bow down" before] a more exalted authority. One who cannot or will not bow, who does not understand the prerogatives of power, can never wield power effectively. The snake, by its refusal to accept God's dictates, by refusing to bow before His will, showed itself unsuitable for kingship and had to forfeit its spine, the mark of its royalty. From now on it would slither along the ground, ominously and menacingly, its erstwhile dignified stance only a mocking memory.

A man who is unable to bring himself to bow when he recites the *modim* blessing[10] has shown himself to be equally unqualified for rulership. In the end, the very spine which was his rod of empire will turn into an undulating snake.

There we have it. We must learn the skill of keeping a "straight spine" while at the same moment prostrating oneself before a higher power. Some anonymous copywriter in an advertising agency got it just right when, many years ago, he produced this wonderful slogan for the Police Athletic League, an organization dedicated to getting children off the streets: Man Never Stands So Straight As When He Stoops To Help a Boy. Beautiful, is it not?

RAV HUTNER'S PARTING DIRECTIVE

What is the bottom line of our *chinuch* enterprise? What do we actually want at the end of the day, after T'NaCh has been taught, dikduk has been [kind of] mastered, the skills for a life-long involvement with *gemara* have been honed in our sons, the seeds for a love of *halachah le'maaseh* have been sown, essential secular disciplines have been offered, the awareness of the need constantly to strive for *gadlus* inculcated and the primacy of being a *mentsch* has been duly impressed by lesson and example upon our students? Which basic quality defines the *Ben Torah* or the *Yiddishe Tochter* whom we want to see growing up to be our future?

The late Rav Chaim Segal, who was for many years the *Menahel* of the High School attached to Yes'ivas Rabbeinu Chaim Berlin, asked this question of Rav Hutner, shortly before the latter's untimely death.

The answer, as reported by Rav Segal in a lecture given some years ago at Ner Israel in Baltimore, was as follows: Teach them this: אשר בחר בנו מכל העמים, *Who has chosen us from among all the nations.* Teach them that we are different and that we are special.[11]

Rav Segal explained why just this idea was uppermost in Rav Hutner's mind. He was thinking of the insidious manner in which the values that hold currency in our host society penetrate banefully and destructively into our own way of thinking. It makes little difference whether the melting pot or the salad bowl is the ideal which currently animates social thinking. Both concepts, and all the many paths and eddies along which they spread and flow, hold one very special concept dear. Everyone is equal before the law,[12] and discrimination on the basis of the many significant differences which the Torah teaches, are forbidden[13]. If we are not very careful, we can easily find ourselves, and particularly our children, somewhat uncomfortable to be seen hanging around a concept like being an עם הנבחר, a chosen people, an ideal which is the very life-blood of our Yiddishkeit.

Rav Hutner knew, and knew well, of what he spoke. *Es iz schwer to zein a Yid in America!*[4]

A LITTLE CHUMASH AND A LITTLE DIKDUK

Rav Hutner's guidance was custom-made for our times. Not ever before the American *galuth*, have conditions been so congenial and discrimination so minimal. Never before did we need a conscious effort to avoid lulling ourselves into oblivion.

We are living through a very, very tiny slice of history. We can view our times as no more than a tiny blip on the giant screen on which the bloody centuries of our agony are etched to eternity.

And yet our generation seems to carry grave import for our People. We are not simply an anonymous mass of incipient lemmings bent on self-destruction. As we shall see, an entire *parashah* in the Torah deals specifically and exclusively with our unique predicament. אין המצוה נקראת אלא על שם גומרה, a mitzvah is ultimately identified only with the one who brings it to fulfillment and fruition [see Sotah 13b]. We, and not our much holier and more worthy ancestors, are the ones who will shortly go out to meet Moshiach. The burden of vindicating the Jewish past, which was forged during two thousand dreadful years of *galuth*, apparently rests on our frail shoulders.

Let us learn a little Chumash. Ramban teaches that the confrontation between Yaakov and Eisav, which is described in VaYishlach, foreshadows our exile experience among Eisav's descendants.[15] Bereishis Rabba (78:15) goes so far as to report that Rav Yannai, whenever he was to have any dealings with the non-Jewish government under which he lived, would prepare himself by studying this *parashah*.

It stands to reason that the last scene in the drama, the interaction which takes place just before the final parting of the ways, would hint at what is to happen at the point at which our *galuth* is about to wind down and enter its final throes. The unique challenge which we and only we must face and the prescription for how we are to deal with it, must be encrypted in those few tantalizing verses, lending us guidance and hope if we can but find it.

Let us learn a little about a few of those verses:

> And he [Eisav] said, "Let us travel and move on. I will make my speed according to your needs [ואלכה לנגדך]."
>
> But Jacob said, "My lord knows that the children are frail and the sheep and cattle, still in the developing stage of their growth, require my care [עלות עלי, (Hirsch)]. Push them beyond their capabilities for even one day, and all the sheep will die."
>
> "Let my Lord go ahead of his servant and I אתנהלה לאטי at a speed suit-

able to the needs of the flock the responsibility for which I bear [אשר עלי], and according to the needs of the children, until I come to my lord in Seir."

[I have provisionally left אתנהלה לאטי, the expression which we will analyze most closely, untranslated.

As in all attempts to render a text into a different language, there is much that must be left to the intuitive sense of the translator. I have supplied the Hebrew in cases in which my translation could be disputed. For example, ואלכה לנגדך could be rendered, I will proceed alongside you [נגד taken its more usual sense as *opposite*]. However, I think it more likely that the phrase here is idiomatic and neither need it nor should it be translated literally. Rashi appears to have understood the phrase as I have translated it.

I have tried to render the passage in a way that would reflect most closely the ideas which, as I adumbrate them below, seem to be expressed by this passage.]

Eisav's offer is redolent with apparent good-will. Nothing in it suggests the man who had earlier been ready to do battle with four hundred men at his command. It would seem that Yaakov's strategy of displaying a fawning subservience had precisely hit the mark and had succeeded in disarming Eisav's anger. A fresh and more friendly atmosphere pervades the scene.

It is Eisav at his most dangerous. Earlier, Yaakov had prayed that God would save him, מיד אחי מיד עשו, "... from the hands of my brother, from the hands of

Eisav." This could well be interpreted as indicating Yaakov's awareness that there were different kinds of weapons in Eisav's arsenal. He could appear as "Eisav," Yaakov's sworn enemy, or as a "brother" oozing fraternal love designed to smother and ultimately to obliterate. Yaakov declines Eisav's offer.

There we have it. *Galuth* America![16]

With unbelievable perspicacity, the Midrash lends additional depth to this passage.[17]

The prize which Yaakov and Eisav had struggled for within their mother's womb was possession of the two "worlds": עולם הזה, this world and עולם הבא, the next. Neither won the battle and each was given only one of the two -- Yaakov the world to come and Eisav the physical world as we know it. When Eisav suggested to Yaakov that they travel together, he meant בשוה in absolute equality (Rashi). Clearly, if Yaakov [who, under the old division, has no portion in עולם הזה except on Eisav's sufferance] can only function as Eisav's guest, that equality would be a sham. Accordingly, the Midrash understands Eisav's offer in a much wider sense than the words would seem to yield. Eisav is actually offering Yaakov to go halves with him in the possession of עולם הזה. The original division is to be voided and both worlds are to be split equally between both of them. Yaakov rejects the offer.

Eisav tries to persuade Yaakov to accede to his suggestion: Are you not afraid of שעבוד מלכיות, the dreadful exile experience which awaits you if you choose to remain the eternal stranger in this my beautiful world?

Yaakov answers that indeed he fears nothing at all. He will make his way slowly and unagressively through history, bowing low to let the raging storms pass over him. He will not allow his children to become citizens in an alien world that is unremittingly hostile to the values which he treasures for them.[18]

How do the insights of the Midrash translate into our little sliver of Jewish experience? Let us return to the Torah text which we quoted above. We had left אתנהלה לאטי untranslated. We need to grapple with this key phrase now.

Let us first deal with אתנהלה.

The use of the *hispa'el*, the reflexive form of the verb, נהל is unique to our passage. The verb is usually in *pi'el*, the intensive active form, and means to lead, to bring to pasture and the like. How does logic require us to understand the word in the *hispa'el*? We cannot render it "to be lead", for that could be conveyed by a simple passive form. Therefore: To have one's mode of leadership imposed upon one by the needs of those whom one must lead.

We lay אתנהלה aside for the moment and go to לאט. Rashi and Radak disagree about the root word from which this form is derived. Rashi thinks לאט, which would mean that the ל is a radical, that it is not a preposition but part of the root. Radak [see Sefer

HaShorashim] derives the word from אט or אטט and treats the ל in our phrase as a preposition.[19]

This allows us to render the phrase such that the *hispa'el* form of אתנהלה is fully utilized. Thus: The form which my leadership is to take will be determined by the measured order imposed upon me [לאטי] by the frailty of my children and the needs of my flock.

In short, by turning down Eisav's offer of citizenship in the transient world which bounds the pathetic lungings for power and meaning which punctuate his sorry existence, Yaakov maintains control. He will not be swept up by current fads and lusts. Only his childrens' needs, expressed as the frailty of the immature unguided and unhelped mind, will determine the form of his life, his hopes, his dreams and his actions.[20] And, of course, they will give direction to the educational system with which he will rear his children.

We have learned the secret which will make it possible for us to survive this final, and in many ways particularly difficult, phase of our *galuth*. It is called *control*.

We stand separate. We must stand separate. Our only hope is to cling mightily to our precious אשר בחר בנו. We can do right by our children, if we do it right.

HOW DO WE GO ABOUT IT?

Ah, if only I knew! I am not foolish enough to think that I can sit at my computer and solve *chinuch* problems. Perhaps it can be done to some extent. There are excellent books by people who, by dint of much thought and serious reflection, have made themselves experts in this fiendishly difficult field. They proffer solid advice that can guide and sometimes help. I am not one of them.

So what is this book about? It offers some thoughts about beauty.

FIGHTING BEAUTY WITH BEAUTY

Let me explain. I am sitting here writing this little essay just a few days after we lit the final eight lights of Chanukah. I will tell you what they said to me. They spoke to me of beauty.

The Gemara [Shabbos 21b] teaches that to fulfill our basic obligation, only one person in the family needs to light one light on each night of Chanukah. But there are other options. The מהדרין, those intent on beautifying the mitzvah beyond what is obligatory, may arrange to light one light per night per person. Those who wish to be מהדרין מן המהדרין, people who insist on taking beauty as far as it can take them, may have every person light each night, not only the indispensable single light but an increasing [or, according to Bais Shammai, a decreasing] number of lights as each day comes and goes.

That is what we do. For Chanukah at least, we are all מהדרין מן המהדרין.

Why the stress on beauty on just this Yom Tov?[21] There are probably many explanations. The following occurred to me this year.

The struggle which we undertook against the Yevanim was one in which beauty was the prize. Hellenistic culture was well nigh irresistible. The grace of the athlete, the profound vision of the consummate artist come alive in the statuary, the stimulating debates, the drama, the poetry and song; they all added up to an ethos alive with charm and promise. Thousands of our best youth were mesmerized. They forsook us in droves, pursuing what they perceived as a spirit-cleansing freedom. May God forgive them their myopia.

The whole thing sounds dreadfully familiar, doesn't it?

There was only one thing to do. Beauty had to be fought with beauty. The military victory would have been almost pointless if, in the end, we would not have been able to hold on to our searching youth. They had to be introduced to the splendor of holiness. Their search for beauty was to be encouraged, but shaped to find the eternal rather than the ephemeral, the authentic rather than the ultimately spurious.

That is what this little book is all about. It attempts to describe a process that may lead us, and through us our children, to a life which is pleasing and admirable. Turn to the last chapter if you like, and read the section entitled *In Benei Berak*. You will know what I mean.

Let us finish with the Midrash Rabba (VaYikra 2:5).

> An artisan was fashioning a crown for the king. A passer-by asked him what he was doing. He explained his purpose.
>
> His interlocutor urged him to spare no ornament that could appropriately be added to the crown. Precious stones, pearls, any object that would enhance its appearance. It was to be worn by the king and for the king nothing can be too beautiful.
>
> Thus did God say to Moshe: The more you can hang ornaments onto the Jewish people, the more you sing their praises and describe their royal dignity, the better will I be pleased. For they are the crown which will ultimately lend me glory. As it is written: And He said to me, "You are My servant. You are Israel through whom I will declare the luster of My majesty." (Yeshayahu 49:3).

OF PARENTS AND PENGUINS

אמר רבי יוחנן אילמלא לא נתנה תורה
היינו למדים צניעות מחתול וגזל מנמלה
ועריות מיונה דרך ארץ מתרנגול...

R' Yochanan taught: Even if the
Torah had not been given, we
would have learned propriety from
the cat; self-sufficiency from the ant;
chastity from the dove and decency
from the hen... (Eruvin 100b)

PARENTS AND CHILDREN

OF EAGLES PENGUINS AND WASPS

Let us once more learn the piece of gemara with
which we headed this chapter.

R' Yochanan taught: Even if the Torah had
not been given, we would have learned
propriety from the cat; self-sufficiency from
the ant; chastity from the dove and decency from the hen... (Eruvin 100b)

Clearly, the animal world has some very important lessons to teach us. What about parenting? Can it help us with that too?

We are all familiar with Rashi (Exodus 19:4): ...the eagle carries its young on its wings. All other birds carry their chicks between their feet because they fear the birds that fly above them. But the eagle, flying higher than any other bird fears only man. Let the arrow pierce me, it thinks, rather than my young.[1]

This is love at its most altruistic.

Let us consider loyalty.

The natural environment of the emperor penguin is the sea; dry land offers it no food. When it is time to mate, the male and female leave the water and trek inland, sliding along icy and forbidding crevices to the mating grounds which may lie some one hundred and thirty kilometers from the sea. It is a trip which can take a month. Once arrived they couple and the female lays an egg. The male takes the egg, puts it on his feet, warms it under the folds of his belly -- and waits. It waits two months, enough time for the female to go back to the sea, gorge itself on fish, and return ready to nurture the chick which has by now emerged. Two months of waiting, two months of starving, drawing only upon its own fat deposits to generate some warmth in the frigid Antarctic night.

This is devotion at its most altruistic.

The solitary wasp labors mightily to build its nest and to lay in an ample food supply for its young. When all is ready she lays her eggs, encloses the nest and flies away, never to see the young which in the course of time will be hatched.

This is nurturing at its most altruistic.

Could R' Yochanan not have taught, that even if the Torah had not been given we could have derived the forms of ideal parental love from the animal world? Perhaps not.

Let us try to find out what the Torah, now that it has been given, teaches us about the parent-child relationship.

A STAFF FOR THE HAND, A SPADE FOR BURIAL

Yevamos 65b teaches that a woman may enter a plea for divorce against a husband who is unable to have children. This, although she is not bound by the Torah command to be fruitful and multiply. The halachah recognizes her claim that, "I need a staff for my hand, a spade for burial." To grow old alone and unhelped is a curse. She has the right to demand the chance to have a child as an insurance against the infirmities of old age.

The plea falls strangely upon our ears. The claim appears to be based on an altogether too utilitarian view of a woman's craving for a child. Must it be concern for the loneliness of the twilight years which gives her plea standing in court? What of the here and now; the simple elemental urge for motherhood? Why not the deeply rooted need to bear, to nurture, to love, to matter?

Let us try and learn from Chanah and her mighty struggle against the barrenness that so blighted her life. What thoughts animated her silent prayer as she stood before God at Shiloh?

Chazal allow us a peek behind the scenes.

Ribono shel Olam! There is nothing in my body which You created without purpose. I see with my eyes, I hear with my ears, I smell with my nose and speak with my mouth. I do work with my hands and walk with my feet. My woman's body was endowed with the capability of producing milk and nursing a child. Is all that to go unused? (Berachos 31b).

This prayer seems to be much more in line with what we would have expected. No mention here of sticks and spades. Chanah argues that a woman's very body screams out for fulfillment. Nature, which is never wasteful, has endowed her body with parts, her soul with needs, which ought not to be denied.

God, as we know, listened to her prayer. Why then should the courts be less sympathetic? Why do they require a claim which is so much more pedestrian, so much less in tune with the rhythms and music of a woman's life?[2]

However, things are not quite so simple.

At the very moment when she is plagued by the terror that her maternal cravings might be permanently frustrated, Chanah makes an offer to God. If He grants her a son she will make a gift of him to HaShem. She will send him to Shiloh to be brought up by Eli the Kohen Gadol and will deny herself the very nurturing role for which, only now, she has so passionately pleaded. It is true that she will send him only after he has been weaned; it is true that her body's potential will have come into its own. But is there not much more than physical nourishment which only a mother's love, a mother's understanding, can give a child? Could Chanah really have thought that her deep longings could be assuaged by so little?

Clearly, then, even a simple reading of the story would seem to yield that Chanah was not driven by her need to nurture and to love[3]. We seem to be back at the stick and the spade. Apparently, she was only concerned with the frustration of her purely physical urges.

How are we to understand all this?

THE "I" OF THE STORM

The truth is that parenthood, as it appears in the Torah, looks very different from the picture which we have drawn from our observations of the animal world. Let us listen carefully and learn what we can learn.

The initial childlessness of Sarah, Rivkah and Rachel is one of the great themes of Sefer Bereishis. Chazal point out a pattern. Why were our forebears barren? Because God craves the prayers of the righteous (Yevamos 64a).

And so we know that they prayed. We do not know, however, the contents of their prayers.

Except for Abraham.

God had appeared to him and promised him untold reward for all that he had done (Bereishis 15:1 and onwards). Abraham finds it difficult to rejoice:

ויאמר אברהם, ה' אלהים מה תתן לי ואנכי הולך ערירי...
ויאמר אברהם,...הן לי לא נתתה זרע והנה בן ביתי יורש אותי.

And Abraham said, "HaShem Elokim: What can You
give me seeing that I pass through life, *ariri?...* "
And Abraham said, "See, to me You have given no
offspring; and see, my steward inherits me!"

Abraham said this and Abraham said that. Two distinct arguments, each able to stand on its own. The second is clear and to the point. Without offspring, there will be no heir within his own family. The golden future which God had promised for his descendants will never come about. It is a point well made and God immediately addresses it. "That one will not inherit you. Only he that shall come forth from within you shall inherit you."

What is Abraham's first point? It all depends on an accurate rendering of *ariri* which we have purposely left in the original. To translate it as *childless* ignores the nuances of the Hebrew wording[4].

Let us do a little sleuthing to find as accurate a meaning as possible. At 17:6, Jeremiah talks of the fate that awaits a person who puts his trust in man, having turned his heart away from God. He will end up like an ערער on the plain. What is an ערער?

Rashi quotes Menachem who believes that it is simply the given name of a tree. Rashi himself favors a different interpretation. The word implies lonesomeness. ערער is not a proper noun but a descriptive phrase. It offers the lone tree as a metaphor for the disillusionment which will bedevil the fool who put his trust in human allies. He will be sorely disappointed. When the chips are down, none of his vaunted allies will be around to help. He will be exposed to the dangers which he had feared and from which he had sought protection, much as a lone tree in the plain is exposed to the elements. Thus, ערער. As proof for his interpretation, Rashi adduces, *ariri*. ערירי describes the state of being alone.

When Abraham, in his first argument, pronounced himself to be *ariri*, he was describing the dreadful sense of isolation which is the lot of the childless man.[5]

Ramban in commenting on Bereishis 15:2 gives a graphic expression to the loneliness expressed in ערירי. "...What value Your gifts as long as I am childless? I wander alone in a strange land, isolated like the *arar* of the plain. No children enliven my home by their comings and goings. Only Eliezer comes into my house, and he is no more than a stranger come to me from Damascus."

Rashi, in commenting on the Bereishis passage, in contrast to his interpretation to Jeremiah, takes the term to describe destruction. Abraham tells God that no amount of reward will mean anything to someone whose life, unblessed by children, lies in ruins.

It would seem that while the second ויאמר אברהם bemoans a blighted future, the first one weeps a stunted present. There is no joy in his home, no sense of a promise that can outlive his own physical frailty. There are only doomed aspirations and a life in ruins.

Abraham's sorrow is a very human one[6]. He craves companionship and the chance to dream. Only children can turn a house into a home, only they can allow us to touch immortality.

Abraham himself, at least in the first of his two protestations, stands at the center of his concerns. He craves children as a fulfillment of his own life.

Human parenting, then, is not altruistic in the sense that animal parenting is. There is, there must always be, the "I" at the center of the storm. [7]

Let us look a little further.

LET THE ARROW PIERCE ME

There is another father-child model upon which we have not yet touched. בנים אתם לה' אלהיכם, You are children of HaShem, your God (Deuteronomy 14:1). God is our father, we are his children.

What does this description say of God's relationship to us, of our relationship to Him?

הלא הוא אביך קניך הוא עשך ויכוננך, Is He not your father Who made you, He created and established you (Deuteronomy 31:6)! In this passage, we are blamed for being derelict in our sense of responsibility, not for being deaf to the music of love. God as our father may make demands, we as His children are bound by duties. No mention here of the softer, joy-filled obligations which, just as insistently, bind a child to a caring and concerned parent.

And yet love is also there, a real, very real love. As we shall see, it has its own halachic implications.

Let us examine some of the implications of the earlier phrase which we cited above: You are children of HaShem, your God. This was said in the context of the prohibition against slashing or otherwise disfiguring oneself in mourning. We are enjoined from such a show of grief because we are God's children.

What has the one to do with the other?

Let us go first of all to Rashi: "Do you not disfigure yourselves as do the Emorites, because you are God's children and it behooves you to be of good appearance, not slashed or balded." Not, we note, as God's servants who have no right to wound themselves, but as God's children who would not wish to have their appearance reflect anything but their joy in being what they are.

We move to Ibn Ezra: "Since you know yourselves to be God's children, [and know] that He loves you more than does a father his son, do not disfigure yourselves, be your fate never so terrible. For whatever He does, He does for the best -- even if you are unable to understand."

Ramban cites Ibn Ezra with approval and then addresses the first phrase in the next verse, ... for you are a holy people to HaShem your God .... He writes: "This assertion [that we are a holy people] carries the promise of immortality in Olam HaBa. The sense is as follows: Since you are a holy people and very special to God ... and since He will certainly make quite sure that not a single one of you will be irredeemably lost, it is inappropriate for you to disfigure yourselves in [exaggerated] mourning, even for someone who dies in his youth ...".

The thread which runs through all these interpretations is a sense of warmth and caring. The mood is one of persuasion, not of demand. We are bidden to sense how special we are to God, how much He cares about us. We are called upon not to dissipate our unique standing in an orgy of self-indulgent mourning.

Our loss is to be measured against that which we cannot lose, our self-absorption is to give way to a more sober, more considered appraisal of who and what we really are.

Very clearly, we matter very much to God.

Just how much we matter to Him is expressed in Rashi's exegesis of Exodus 19:5 and 6. The provenance of this passage is clearly the need to prepare the Children of Israel for the enormity of the commitment which they are about to make as they accept the Torah which God is proffering to them.

Here is what God says:

"Egyptian depravity could have elicited divine retribution long before Israel ever came to their land. But they were never touched. They were simply too insignificant. It was only when they became entangled in Jewish history, became arbiters of Jewish fate, that they became of concern and, therefore, a target for divine interference. We and only we are God's *segulah* -- His special love and thus the logical focus of His active concern."

Here we have the introduction to Mattan Torah. From a pedagogical perspective it makes much sense. We need to know how beloved we are. Certainly we need to know this if we are to shoulder the heavy yoke of Torah. But pedagogy is not enough. We must be wary of so diminishing God's words as to read them in the narrow, manipulative sense which lurks behind the dictionary meaning of the term.

We should perhaps understand the passage as follows: The Torah which God is about to give us, the heavy, heavy yoke which He is about to place upon our willing shoulders, is to be a gift of love.

We know that we can know nothing of God. We know that we must make use of anthropomorphisms if we are to grasp anything at all. Nonetheless, knowing nothing, this we know -- that if this were a human father about to bestow such servitude upon his child, if there were a moment between them as pregnant with heart-breaking ecstasy as this, if a human father could foresee for his son a destiny fraught with so much dreadful pain, with so many dreadful longings, if martyrdom in the grand and sweeping scale of our history were in the balance, and if he knew that he could trust his child to grasp at this proffered greatness -- then that father's heart would ache with a burning love.

'Let the arrow pierce me.' he might have said, 'O that I could bear the pain in place of my child!'

THE WILL TO SURVIVE,
THE DETERMINATION TO LIVE

Let us tell the tale of the seventeen-year cicada. Precisely every seventeen years, much of the United States is infested with millions upon millions of locusts.

You cannot escape the monotonous sound of their whirring wings. You crunch them underfoot as you walk the streets; they cover the trees with a clammy treacle-like substance -- and you wish they were not there.

Why are they?

As far as we can see, there is only one reason, and that is to survive. The short period during which they are above ground gives them the chance to mate, to fertilize, to produce eggs from which nymphs are hatched in order to guarantee another generation. For this they wait seventeen long and dark years in the ground. For this they shoulder their grim destiny. Only survival is their purpose, only this their justification.

This appears to be the inexorable law of the natural world. Its watchword is the יהי with which God brought it into being. It is that word and no other which demands that the chameleon change its colors, which speeds the deer along its path, lends the turtle its shell, the lion its roar, and the fox its cunning.

To be, to continue to be, to survive -- that is the great imperative. In the context of this imperative, the species reigns supreme. The individual is the means, never the end. Immediately after fertilization, the male spider is gobbled up by the female and see! nature smiles. His life's work has been fulfilled; he will live on in the brood.[8]

CHANAH'S STRUGGLE

Man, the midrash tells us, is composed of two opposing elements. He combines within himself the עליונים, the realm of the spirit, and the תחתונים, the absolute physical [See Rashi to Genesis 2:7].

There is much in our physiology which we share with the animals. We hunger, we lust, we crave sleep and comfort in much the same way as they do. In all these matters, it is that part of us which belongs to the *tachtonim* which comes into play. The control which we exercise, our ability to lift ourselves beyond these needs -- these call upon the royal reach of the *elyonim*.

In essence, the craving to bear, to nurture, to mother, is no different from that same urge that is manifest in the lower orders. The heights of heroism and self-denial which can be, and often are, manifested, may be no more than an instinctive obeisance to the *yehi* of all creation, to the preeminence of the species over the individual. It is noble, but it is instinctive. It does not call upon the distinctly human. It is in no way rooted in the Tzelem Elokim. When that comes into play, the results may well be the very opposite of those which instinct would have prompted.

The needs which drive our prayers are often the most elemental stirrings of our being. We can borrow the thought from Iyov: מבשרי אחזה אלוה, "It is from my flesh that I learn to behold God." Chanah's dreadful,

aching, need for a child drew its provenance from the
ringing יהי of creation. Her shriveling body was mute
testimony to a life without a future, a stunted aberration
in a world bursting with the joy of promise[9]

Chanah nevertheless knew better than to identify
with her physical longings, natural and legitimate though
they were. Her body may have goaded her to prayer, but
it was her soul that had the final say, which determined
what would be done if that prayer were answered. She
would rise above her primeval longings, stifle her nurturing instinct and give her child to God.

BACK TO THE STICKS

We are now in a better position to understand
why the cravings for motherhood seem to have no
standing in the courts. The helplessness of a destitute
old age is an objective, societal problem with which
justice must deal. The husband, his rights and his
feelings, innocent though he may be of any wrongdoing,
must yield to his wife's demonstrable need of a "stick for
the hand, a spade for burial". By contrast, the woman's
desperate longing for a child, natural though it is, fierce
and unyielding though it may be, can, and therefore
must, be subdued in the face of the loyalties demanded
by the bonds of marriage; therefore they remain legally
unactionable.

WE ARE NOT PENGUINS

We began our analysis by wondering why, in our own parenting, we are not exhorted to emulate the selflessness displayed by animals towards their young.

The parenting patterns of the animal world ought to teach us nothing at all. They are prompted by the primordial drive to self-perpetuation through the species, and lead to the total self-sacrifice of the parent to the child. This can never be a model for us. Such an attitude would diminish our humanity, would submerge our Tzelem Elokim into an anonymous mass of insignificant nonentities. We must never allow this to come about.[10]

We are not here for our children and our children are not here for us. Each of us, fathers as well as sons, have our own wars to wage, our own secrets to unravel. Each of us must ultimately struggle on his own; each must create the harmonies and dissonances which will set his particular and unparalleled life to music. To seek fulfillment through our children, to delude ourselves that in their victories our own deficiencies are obliterated, to bask in their accomplishments and thereby feel relieved from the threats and terrors which haunt our own battlefields is nothing but travesty.

Our lodestar is not the יהי which looks always onwards and outwards, which downgrades the individual into a mere handmaiden of the species, but the magisterial נעשה אדם בצלמנו כדמותנו (Genesis 1:26) which whispers of an innate Godliness residing in the uniqueness of each person.[11]

And that is why, as we discovered above, the 'I' is such a ubiquitous presence in the parenting which is projected by the Torah. It is the reflection of a reality which we ignore at our peril. Self-awareness and the examination of all relationships in the light of that 'self' is not a human failing, but the solid and healthy bedrock upon which alone, a life of service to God can be built.

We delude ourselves if we think that we can take ourselves out of the equation. Only God's love can be totally altruistic. Only He can look to the totally selfless eagle as the appropriate metaphor for His relationship to His children[12].

We are not penguins and we are certainly not God. We are here because we have a job to do on ourselves and for ourselves. Long, long before we get to our children, we must educate ourselves. If our lives radiate beauty, our children will learn that beauty is the stuff of life.

Above all, let us learn to live beautifully.

אחד הפקיד אצלי פקדון...

Someone entrusted me
with a deposit

CHILDREN -- FOR DEPOSIT

A MATTER OF TRUST

How does the Torah view the relationship between parents and their children, between children and
their parents?

We go to ch.31 in Midrash Mishley:

> One Shabbos, while R' Meir was
> teaching in the Beis HaMidrash, his two
> sons died. His wife covered them with a
> sheet and laid them down in the attic.
>
> After he came home, had made
> havdalah and eaten, she asked him a ques-
> tion: "Someone entrusted me with a de-
> posit and now asks that I return it to him.
> Do we return it or not?"

He told her that, of course, she was obliged to return the deposit.

Then she showed him his sons. When he began to cry she reminded him of what he had told her. Had he himself not said that a deposit must be returned?

He found comfort in her words.

Parents, then, are mere custodians.[1] When we talk of our children we mean this only in a borrowed sense. They are ours to the extent that they have been entrusted to us. They are a *pikadon*[2]. We are mere *shomrim*[3]. Things are not as simple as we thought.

RESPONSIBLE STEWARDSHIP

Shomrim are in the employ of their depositors (Bava Metzia 81a). There are obligations that must be met, responsibilities that must weigh upon them.

Who is the depositor to whom we must render our efforts? What are his expectations of the stewardship with which he has entrusted us?[4]

Since the child does not deposit himself, there is really only one possibility. It is God Who is the Great Depositor. It is He Who committed His children to our care. It is to Him, finally, that we will have to render an accounting of how well we filled the role of *shomer*.

What are the principles of responsible steward-ship? Let us study the mishnah in Bava Metzia 2:8.

Someone has found an object and is now duty-bound to return it to the owner in the best possible condition. The mishnah delineates his obligations.

> If he found scrolls, let him read in them, or at least roll them, once in thirty days ... If it was a garment, let him shake it out as required and spread it out if that will help, but never for his own use. If he found objects made from silver or copper, let him use them to the extent that it is of benefit to them, but never so much that they become eroded. If they were made of gold or glass, they require nothing at all so let him not touch them.

Clearly, there are limits to what this mishnah can teach us. At bottom, there is no real comparison between our children and a found object. Nevertheless, some broad outlines are apparent:

> 1. Where indicated, there must be periodic exposure to the fresh air if an inner fouling is to be avoided.
> 2. Any action must be solely determined by the needs of the child. Our own gratifi-

cation may not play any role at all in determining what ought to be done.

3. Different children require different degrees of attention. Not everything that is of benefit to one will be good for another.

4. Too much of a good thing can eventually prove to be destructive. Watch out for erosion!

5. If nothing needs to be done, don't do it.

Each of these principles will require our attention. They constitute the skeletal structure over which we must tug and stretch the specific and highly individualized chinuch that we give each of our children.

GUARDIANSHIP IN ACTION

The cardinal sin of the *shomer* is פשיעה, carelessness. We have a responsibility to act responsibly.

Let us apply some of the principles that we have now learned.

1. Where indicated, there must be periodic exposure to the fresh air if an inner fouling is to be avoided.

This is a hard one. It may go against the grain, and if it is to work correctly it must be precision-timed and calibrated. But it is important.

Let us listen to HaRav Shimshon Rafael Hirsch, one of the premier educators of our times, the man who saved a generation with his pedagogical insights. Perhaps not everyone would agree, but the idea is worthy of consideration.

Let us listen, learn and think.

Immediately prior to Isaac's birth, Abraham left his home of many years to take up residence in the inhospitable Southland [ארץ הנגב]. He settled in the desert [בין קדש ובין שור] with only occasional and temporary visits to Gerar [ויגר בגרר], the capital city of the Philistines [See Genesis 20:1]. No reason is ascribed to this move.

Hirsch surmises as follows: In his own religious development, Abraham had passed from an earlier stage in which he preferred the isolation of desert life [see Hirsch at 12:8] to a point at which he intermingled freely and productively with his friends, Aner, Eshkol and Mamreh. Now, however, in anticipation of Isaac's birth, he decided once more to move into the wilderness where, away from the distractions of city life, he could protect his child from the pernicious influences of the prevailing and pervasive culture.

The isolation, however, was not to be complete.

With exquisite sensitivity, Abraham realized that total seclusion is rarely healthy. Just as an overprotective mother virtually guarantees that her child will catch cold at first exposure to a breath of fresh air, so too can a religious rigidity which never allows a child to observe -- and reject -- other ideas, make him vulnerable when he becomes buffeted by the howling gales of religious pluralism, dilettantism, and often, too often, outright antagonism.

Where does one go? Where could balance be maintained without undue risk?

The Philistines had never sunk to the depths of depravity in which the Canaanites wallowed. Abraham felt that a judicious, controlled and temporary exposure to their lives would allow Isaac to make the appropriate comparisons in relative safety and thus guarantee that he would never want to stray from his own destiny.

Abraham chose to dwell in the desert, but made sure that occasional forays into Gerar remained optional. As parents, we too will have to make choices.

Occasionally the prevailing culture may be so baneful, and its ramifications perceived as so negative, that the only safe reaction, from an educational standpoint, is a ruthless denigration of even its positive aspects. Sometimes the grays are simply too threatening, and we become reduced to a distorted insistence upon blacks and whites which reflect no truth, but promise a degree of safety.[5]

When this is the case, we would do well to hermetically seal our homes and shoulder the risks which inhere in such an isolated upbringing. It is, after all, better to risk a case of the sniffles than a full-fledged medical crisis.

If this is our judgment, however, we had better be sure that we are right. In the short term, such isolationism may well seem justified. Unchallenged by competing values, children will readily intuit what is expected of them and blend into the value system which we favor, probably with little opposition.

In the long run, however, things are not so certain. Hot-house plants wilt easily in a hostile environment.

God the Depositor will want to know whether, where indicated, we exposed His *pikadon* to the elements. The path of least resistance may be strewn with some very threatening boulders as it winds its way through life.

2. Any action must be solely determined by the needs of the child. Our own gratification may not play any role at all in determining what ought to be done.

We look at our children and tend to see ourselves. They lend glow to our aging, vigor to our infirmities, sparkle to our blandness and hope to our terrors. They hold mortality at bay. They whisper of a future of which, without them, we might have despaired. They allow us to believe in dreams that may yet come true, in ultimate vindication where without them there would be, so we may feel, nothing at all.

It is so easy to look upon them as objects rather than as subjects, as extensions of ourselves rather than as discrete personalities with needs and predilections of their own. It is easy to forget that their dreams and ambitions may have very little to do with those that we have for them.

How wrong is such a view? To what extent are we justified in looking upon our children as factors in our own lives, meaningful, first and foremost, to ourselves?

Let us think about names. Ibn Ezra in Sefer HaShem claims that the Hebrew, שם [vocalized with tzeirei] meaning *name*, is related to שם [vocalized with *kamatz*], meaning *there*. We could understand this as follows: The name, as it were, locates the person or object to which it is attached, for the one assigning the name. For him, in the periphery of his individual vision, the designated person or object is specifically 'there' and not somewhere else. He or it plays this role and not that and represents, for him at least, this idea and no other.

And it is true that in the Torah, in most cases where reasons are assigned, names appear to have been given with the parents' perspective in mind. They have, as it were, attached a defining location relative to themselves.

Nevertheless, there appears to be another way of naming a child.

Shemos Rabba notes how great is the reward of those who deal kindly with people. Moses had many names, but of all of them the Torah uses only משה, the one given to him by Pharaoh's daughter.

This midrash is based upon the Sages' understanding of I Chronicles 4:18, where the names of the children of the Egyptian princess Bisiah are listed. In reality, so the Sages interpret, there was only one son, Moses, 'born' to Pharaoh's daughter in the sense that she raised him as her own child. The various names listed in the verse are all ones by which he was known.

One of the names is Chever [from חבר, to join], assigned to Moses by his father, Amrom, because it was through this child that he had been reunited to his wife whom he had previously divorced. Another was Yekuthiel [from קוה, to hope or to anticipate]. This name was given to Moses by his mother who, even after she had consigned him to the river, never ceased to hope that he would one day be returned to her. Another was Yered [from ירד, to go down], given by Miriam as a reminder that it was because of him that she had gone down to stand by the river in order to learn of his fate (See Yalkut Shimoni, Shemos 166).[6]

Why then was the name משה chosen from among all these possibilities? The answer suggested by the midrash that we quoted above ascribes this to the kindness of Bisiah. But the midrash does not explain which act of kindness is meant and, moreover, does not make clear why calling the child by the name that she had given rather than by any other, is an appropriate reward.

We suspect that the kindness that the midrash refers to is one which Bisiah expressed in the naming of the child. This as follows:

The Torah explains the name משה [from משה, to draw out] because, "I drew him out of the water." But, as Midrash Lekach Tov and Sforno point out, the form that the name takes seems inconsistent with this meaning. משוי, the passive voice, is the correct form to describe someone who has been drawn out. משה, in the active voice, describes one who is performing the rescue.

The answer offered is as follows: Bisiah realized that the providential circumstances under which she found the child pointed to a very specific destiny. This little boy who had been saved would one day be called upon to save others. He would snatch them from the savage grasping waters even as he had been snatched out before it was too late.

So why immortalize this destiny in his name? It seems to me that Bisiah wanted to teach this child, who had now become her very own, a lesson for life. Someone had helped him; someone had, at the crucial moment, stretched out a hand when he needed it most. Let him now help others, let his hand be extended in friendship and concern. To be a משוי was not sufficient. That name would have celebrated history and taught nothing at all concerning life. Bisiah summoned him to become a משה.

And so the Torah rejected Amrom's Chever, Yocheved's Yekuthiel and Miriam's Yered. The שם [vocalized with *kamatz*, meaning there] of those names, the position that they assigned to the child upon whom they bestowed them, was located within the periphery of their own concerns. Only Bisiah managed to distance herself entirely. Had she wanted a memento of this most significant moment in her life, she would have named the child משוי. The name משה places the child firmly and unambiguously at center stage.

Bisiah became the paradigm of ideal parenthood. Biology plays less a role than selfless concern. She had "borne" Moshe because she had raised him. The true parent is the one who equips the child to live his life as God would have him live it (Megillah 13a).

3. Different children require different degrees of attention. Not everything that is of benefit to one will be good for another.

If it has worked once, it may not necessarily work again.

R' Elazar HaKapor's nephew, Chiah, had a beautiful voice. His uncle would urge him to use it as often as he could. He suggested that he should become the *chazan* of the synagogue in which he prayed. God had given him something very special. It made his task in life different from that of his brothers. It would be his duty and fulfillment to use his talent to the utmost (Yalkut Shimoni to Proverbs 3:9).[7]

To uncover natural affinities, to encourage, to nurture, to guide, to direct what is already there -- that is the secret of good educating. We can try to force our children into a mold of our own choosing. We are strong, and they are weak. Our victory, however, will be short-lived. Let the child but escape our control and he will revert to that which nature has decreed.

Thus Gra to Proverbs 22:6: If you want to teach your child lessons that will remain with him throughout his life, then guide him along that path that is in consonance with his *mazal* and his nature. If you try to break him into new paths, fear may be your ally in the short term, but let him just be free of you, and he will shuck off all that is artificial for him. No one can ultimately change his *mazal*.[8]

Our forefather Jacob knew this secret, and before his death, crafted the blessings with which he was to leave his children, so that they would accord with the nature and characteristics of each one of them. Thus Hirsch to Genesis 49:28 that reads: "All these are Israel's tribes, twelve of them, and it is this that their father pronounced concerning them, so that when he blessed them he did so for each in accordance with that blessing which was appropriate to him."

Jacob did not immediately bless his children. That would come only after he had defined for himself each one's discrete character, each one's individual predilections ["... twelve of them"]. First came the דבר להם, only then ויברך אותם. None of his children were absolutely alike; none would be encouraged to become a carbon-copy of the other. To manhandle a Yissachar into becoming a Zevulun, to force a Zevulun into the Yissachar mold -- that would have spelled stark tragedy. The dedicated educator must strive for diversity, never for uniformity.[9]

4. Too much of a good thing can eventually prove to be destructive. Watch out for erosion!

Habit is our friend and our enemy. Bend it to our needs and it serves us well. It frees the mind and makes the most clumsy fingers dance. But give it control and it is lethal. It deadens the soul, shackles the spirit and drives the mind into worn-out grooves of stodgy conformity. It saps resourcefulness and replaces the exercise of divine freedom with a depressing Pavlovian slavering.

The creative use of opposites is where the secret of real living lies.

Herewith a little *d'rush* which, though it might well be stretching the meaning of the text a little (as *d'rush* often does), contains an important grain of truth.

Most of us know Rabbi Yehudah HaLevi's immortal hymn, יום ליבשה נהפכו מצולים.... If we say *piyutim*, we have learned to love it from the Pesach Machzor. If we do not, we have probably heard it sung at a Bris Milah. In it, he admires Israel's virtuosity. למי החותמת ולמי הפתילים Who else is like [this nation]! They posses both the seal [Bris Milah] and the fringes [Tzitzis].

Why just these two? What is so special about a people who adhere to just these mitzvos? The answer, we feel, lies in the fact that these address two opposite and apparently irreconcilable human traits. Circumcision reflects that part of us that wants no truck with compromise, which demands that evil and uncleanliness be excised, that sanctity be wrested from out of a battlefield in which no quarter is given. Tzitzios, on the other hand, speak of sublimation, of the ability to turn the mundane towards heaven. They do not cut but challenge, they do not denigrate but uplift. They speak to the optimist within us[10].

R' Yehudah HaLevi is telling us [or, if we are literal minded, is perhaps hinting to us] that truly happy people are those who are not constricted in their attitudes and actions. They are the ones who react as the moment requires and are not mired in the sloth of debilitating conditioning.[11]

This is what Shlomo HaMelech meant when, in Koheles, ch.3, he spoke of the need to realize that there is an appropriate time for everything and its opposite. If all we can do is to build, we will fall short of living as we should; we must also be able to destroy. Our embraces have meaning only if we have the sense, as the occasion requires, to distance ourselves from embracing.

It is relatively easy to fashion automatons who react predictably to every situation. To raise children who will master their lives is another matter altogether.

5. If nothing needs to be done, don't do it.

The education of our children may be viewed as a function of our own maturity. The ability to occasionally leave well enough alone, to allow flowering and maturing to take their own good time and direction, to be able to retreat into our own zone of privacy and allow our children to enjoy their own; these all take courage. They are not for the faint-hearted and the insecure.

Thus we have a great Rosh Yeshiva's exhortation to a father who was too frequently and compulsively inquiring about his son's progress: "You would not think of constantly digging up a seed to see whether it was growing as it should. You have planted well and wisely. Give the boy some space of his own. If there are problems I will let you know."

מי כמך באלים ה'--מי כמך באלמים, Who is like You among the mighty, O HASHEM! -- Who is like You among those who are silent! (Gittin 56b).

To resist the urge to assert ourselves is perhaps our greatest test. When we manage to be silent, we partake of the Godly.[12]

****

We have taken an important first step towards being good mechanchim. We have learned to ask the right question. We do not ask what we can demand of our children, but what God, the Great Depositor, demands of us.

מנעו בניכם מן ההגיון...

Do not allow your children to lapse into superficiality (Berachos 28b)

FIGHTING THE GOOD FIGHT

THE ARROW AND THE QUIVER

Observe the archer. The steady eye. Power flowing smoothly from bulging muscle to straining bow. The taut string alive with the energy of latent flight. The arrow straight and sure, poised for the grace and beauty of the perfect trajectory.

You have seen a father and his child.

"As arrows in the warrior's hand, so are the children of one's youth. Happy the man who has filled his quiver with them..." (Psalms 127:4-5).

We have met the child as arrow, and the home as quiver. We have learned that parents might be viewed as warriors. Who is the enemy?

The metaphor seems flawed. Instead of remaining consistent to the image with which it began, the psalm suddenly switches to the real world: Happy the man who has filled his quiver with them -- they [the parents] will not be embarrassed when they [the children] debate foes at the gate.

Why not carry the metaphor to its logical conclusion? Why not tell us about the target at which the arrow is directed?

It would appear that the word-picture loses its efficacy at this point. It is the arrow in the archer's hand, the control that he exercises, the aim that he must take with such attention to the subtleties of wind and gravity, the power to propel the projectile along the path that he has chosen, which are to engage our attention.[1] The flight of the arrow to its mark [To wound? To help indulge the vainglory of the marksman?] can evoke no useful resonance in our minds.

And so we send out our children, arrow-like, to confront the enemy at the gate[2]. They are propelled by the brawn of our determination, impelled by the force and urgency of our longing. We want so much to send them straight and true, to guide them along the path that we know to be the right one for them. The psalmist assures us that they will not let us down.

What is the secret? What, above all, can we give our children to guarantee that they will not be an embarrassment to us when life confronts them with its challenges?

LIVING SERIOUSLY

When R' Eliezer [HaGadol, the son of Horkenos] was ill, his students came to visit him[3]. They asked him to to set them on the path which would lead them to eternal life in the World to Come. He had three pieces of advice:

> 1. Be considerate of your friend's dignity.
> 2. Do not allow your children to lapse into superficiality[4]. Make sure that they keep company with the wise.
> 3. When you pray, bear in mind in front of Whom you are standing (Berachos 28b).

There is a sobering thought here. We are to be judged, at least in part and where it matters profoundly, by the job we do in educating our children. If we permit them to skim life's surface instead of plumbing its profundities, we have compromised our own inner integrity. We have strayed from the road by which we must enter Olam HaBa.

Let us then analyze the three maxims of R' Eliezer a little further. We need very much to get them right.

The visit described in this gemara took place on the last day of R' Eliezer's life [see Endnote #3 to this chapter]. This was not, however, the first time that he had attempted to distill his ideas into three aphorisms. Avos 2:9 tells how much earlier, when he was still a student of R' Yochanan ben Zakkai, he, together with four colleagues was challenged by their master to find the path [דרך ישרה] along which a man should choose to make his life.

At that time, he suggested the following:

> 1. Let the dignity of your friend be as dear to you as your own. Do not anger easily.
>
> 2. Repent one day before your death.
>
> 3. Warm yourself by the fire of the wise, while taking care not to be scalded by their coals. For their bite is the bite of a fox, their sting, the sting of the scorpion, their hiss is the hiss of the serpent, and all their words are like fiery coals.

The similarity between the first of the three maxims in both sets is so striking that we are inclined to say that the second and third in each list also parallel one another.

This would yield: Repent one day before your death = Do not allow your children to lapse into superficiality, and: Warm yourself by the fire of the wise... = When you pray, bear in mind in front of Whom you are standing.

Can this theory of congruency be justified? Or are we needlessly locking ourselves into a formal structural symmetry that cannot be sustained without the kind of mental gymnastics that, as reasonable people, we ought to eschew?

Let us begin by analyzing the relationship of the two opening maxims to one another. On his death-bed R' Eliezer said, Be considerate of your friend's dignity. Earlier the language had been stronger: Let the dignity of your friend be as dear to you as your own. The latter formulation demands much less than the earlier one. What has happened?

Clearly, there can be more than one truth. The chal-lenge that can fire the heroes among us, ought not to be thrust upon those with more flabby aspirations. To tantalize with a prize that exceeds our reach is to guarantee a sullen acceptance of failure. We can succeed only by finding the reasonable distance, one which will make us want to stretch our muscles and extend our grasp, but which will not doom our efforts to failure.

As a young scholar, R' Eliezer wanted no truck with the ordinary. His mode was the searing passion of youth. Only the highest hurdle, the fiercest battle could nourish his dreams. The weathered sage was more understanding of our all too human, all too widely distributed frailties. He was willing to talk of a softer dream.[5]

Granted our thesis, we would be justified in suspecting that in the matter of the second and third maxim too, R' Eliezer was addressing a different audience, one to whom the demands of the earlier formulation were just too daunting.

Let us examine the second maxim.[6]

Shabbos 153a puts it in perspective:

> The students asked [R' Eliezer who had advised repenting on the day before death], "Does then a person know when he is going to die?"
>
> R' Eliezer answered, "All the more reason to tell him to repent. Let him be concerned lest he dies tomorrow. Thus will he spend his entire life in penitence."

But what a thing to ask! An entire life lived with the anticipation of death as a constant companion. Living each second as though it were the last. Living in unremitting tension, desperately squeezing each moment for maximum yield. That is a life lived to the utmost. That is life lived seriously![7]

Perhaps too seriously for most. Perhaps here as well, R' Eliezer thought that some downgrading was necessary for the less venturesome.

And so he substituted the second maxim of the second list: Do not allow your children to lapse into superficiality[8]. If we educate our children to the idea that life is serious, that it has depth and that we will not tolerate superficiality, we will have set them on the right path. Who knows? Perhaps with such a *chinuch*, they will one day approximate the ideal of R' Eliezer's dreams. Perhaps they will learn to intuit that life is fleeting -- and serious -- and will repent today lest they die tomorrow.

IT IS EASIER SAID THAN DONE

How do we do it?

The holy Kotzker Rebbe was asked by a chassid what he, as a father, might do to make sure that his son would always take learning Torah seriously. The Rebbe answered, "Make sure that you yourself learn conscientiously. If you do, you will find your son doing just that. If you just keep on worrying about the child, he will grow into a father who is just like you. Instead of learning himself, he will always be worrying about making his children learn."

Our children will live seriously if we do. If we are to be responsible educators, we must become responsible human beings.

In the coming chapters we will examine some areas which may need a little work. Let us be serious about becoming serious in:

Our relationships with Jew and Non-Jew.

Our awareness of our Galuth existence.

Dealing with money.

Dealing with time.

Learning and playing.

Praying.

Dealing with our selves.

לפיכך נברא האדם יחידי...מפני...
שלום הבריות שלא יאמר אדם
לחברו אבא גדול מאביך

It is for this reason that man was created singly...so that we might live in peace with one another; that one should not say to another, "My father is more important than yours." (Sanhedrin 37a).

TAKING RELATIONSHIPS SERIOUSLY

CHILDREN AS MICROPHONES

Do you want to eavesdrop on your neighbors? Listen to their children talk. In the expressions they use, in their tone and in their bearing, you will hear their parents speak.

Miriam, one of the Bilga family, turned her back upon her people and married a Greek general. When the

Greeks entered the Temple she came along with them. Striking the altar, she screamed: "You are no better than a wolf! All you do is gobble up Israel's wealth. You never help them when they need you!"

In reaction to this disgraceful episode, the Sages denied the entire Bilga family certain privileges that they had previously held.

But, should a whole family be penalized for the misdeeds of one daughter?

Abaye said, "Yes, indeed. It is as people say, 'A child's language reflects what he has heard from his parents.'" (Succah 56b)

****

It is Sunday afternoon. We have great plans for catching up on all the work that has piled up during the week. We will make every minute count and, at the end of the day, expect to luxuriate in the knowledge that what was needed to be done had been done. The bell rings. A Jew needs help. And then another and then another. Another pack of needs and sorrows. Perhaps it is הכנסת כלה this time. There is a daughter for whom a wedding must be made. We resent the intrusion, we resent the pressure, we resent the cause. Nobody helps us when our children have to be married.

We all know the story. Our children are watching. They see our faces, observe the glances we exchange. They hear the tone of our greeting. They read the body language that they know so well.

We have just seconds to decide. Their fate as human beings is in our hands. We will make them or break them. A child's language reflects what he has heard from his parents. For all his life, he will carry our attitudes with him!

OF OBJECTS AND SUBJECTS

How exactly are we supposed to relate to others? The Torah has some very radical ideas. We are to regard whomever we meet as our ruler and ourselves as his subject.

How so? Otzar HaMidrashim, Gan Eden Ve-Gehinam, Section 43 teaches that among the questions which we will be asked when we stand before the heavenly tribunal is: "Did you willingly declare your fellow to be king over you [המלכת את חברך בנחת רוח]."

No source is adduced for this shocking statement and it leaves us very shaken.

Why, after all, should I? And if I should, then he too must proclaim me ruler over himself. If he is my ruler and I am his, where does this leave us?

As a heading to this chapter, we quoted the mishnah in Sanhedrin 37a that muses upon the fact that man, alone among all God's creatures, was created singly. The animals, the birds, the fish, the vegetable world, all appeared in their teeming millions, filling the world with all its variegated glory.

Adam was created alone. For what purpose? So that he should live with the sense that, "It is for me alone that the world was created." (Sanhedrin, there)

This is to be man's credo:

I am at the center of my own universe. The people I meet, the events I experience, nature itself in all its vast and fearful mystery, are all objects to my subject. They exist for me only to the extent that I define and classify them. They have significance only to the extent that I am not willing to filter them out of my awareness.

I am absolute king.

But what possible good can such thinking produce? It is this: We are bidden by the mishnah to assert the centrality that is ours in our subjective universe, so that we should realize the pity, futility and wastefulness of sin. We are to conclude that it would be foolish to destroy an entire world [ourselves] for a moment's fleeting pleasure (Rashi, there). That is the practical outcome of the mishnah's ruling.

So what can the Sages have meant when they required that I declare everyone whom I meet as ruler over myself? They meant this: That I am to banish the mishnah's insight into the depths of my heart. That I am to have it form my perception of myself, but never my attitude towards others.

I am to shake myself loose from my tendency to grant people legitimacy only to the extent that they subordinate themselves to my desires. I am to admit, not grudgingly if possible, that if I am ruler in my universe, they are rulers in theirs. The Sages demand that I realize that to the same extent that I am inclined to view them as objects to my subject, they are inclined to view me as object to their subject.

I am to treat all men as equals. I am to eschew manipulation as a legitimate means of dealing with them. I am to recognize the integrity of their discrete and unique claim on life -- their rulership over me within their own domain -- and not impugn it through deceit, disrespect or indifference. They have the right to expect me to see in them the Tzelem Elokim as surely as I expect them to see it in me.

EARNING RESPECT

Who is deserving of respect? He who respects others, as it is said, "For those who honor Me I will honor, but those who scorn Me shall be disdained" (Avos 4:1).

There is a problem here. The mishnah asserts that in order to be deserving of honor we are to honor others. This is well and good. The concept is one that we can grasp[1]. But how is it yielded by the passage that is quoted in support? That verse talks about one who honors God [For those who honor Me ...], not one who shows respect to his fellow man.

The conclusion is inescapable. We honor God when we honor man. We honor in man that aspect of his being which is touched by the divine.

We earn respect, that is, we give weight[2] and significance to the divine within ourselves when we, by our actions and attitudes, allow that same affinity with Godliness to come to the fore in others.

We are, so this mishnah teaches us, to move in a world in which everyone whom we meet is touched by a grace that lifts him beyond the merely human.

It is a strange world. One in which values are turned topsy-turvy; where things are not at all as we would expect them to be.

Let us consider Rambam, Avel 14:1-2:

> Rabbinic ordinance bids us to care for the sick, bring comfort to mourners, bury the dead, share in the joy of weddings, escort our guests as they leave our homes and involve ourselves with all the various aspects of burying the dead...

Of all these, the reward for escorting guests is the greatest. It is a custom instituted by our father, Abraham, and reflects the goodness that informed his life. He would feed travelers, offer them drink and accompany them along their way...

Why should the mitzvah of *levayah* be greater than any other? Logic seems to dictate otherwise. The sick need attention, the dead must be buried, but our guests can get along quite well without our walking them a part of the way.

That, said the late, saintly, R' Dovid Kronglas, is just the point. All those other services that we are bidden to perform address not the person but his needs. They say nothing of the simple grandeur of simply being human. *Levayah* celebrates the man. There is no greater gift.

OF MINDS AND MEN

I am a wine-merchant. I have an order to deliver for which I will have to break open a fresh barrel. A customer enters the store and wants to buy some wine. I walk over to the barrel that I would anyway have had to use, and open it, thus making him think that I am doing it just for him. He feels like a favored customer. He glows with self-importance and feels good towards me.

I am, he now confirms to himself, a merchant after his own heart. Not like some of the others who do not give him the respect that he so richly deserves.

I am a thief. I have not overcharged him; I have not taken a penny that is not justly mine. Nevertheless, I am a thief. I have stolen something infinitely more precious. I have "stolen his mind." I have impinged upon the integrity of his personhood.

I meet a friend. I beg him to come home for a meal, knowing full well that, for whatever reason, he cannot or will not come.

I am a thief. I have not picked his pocket -- but I have violated his mind. And that is worse.

Shmuel taught: It is forbidden to "steal" people's minds [אסור לגנוב דעת הבריות],[3] even that of an idol-worshiper (Chullin 94a).

It is particularly significant that it is Shmuel who taught us that גנבת דעת, 'stealing' the mind, is forbidden even when the victim is the most depraved idol-worshiper. For Shmuel himself had, on occasion, earned a profit from a slip that a gentile idol-worshiper had made. On that occasion, Shmuel felt no sense of moral obligation to tell him of his mistake and return the money (Bava Kama 113b). The man was so corrupt that he had no claim upon Shmuel's good will.

And yet the mind, if not the property, of even such a Rasha, must remain inviolate. Why? Because mind is essence. Because even people who have sunk low enough to have forfeited certain financial protections [see Bava Kama 38a] retain the dignity of their humanity.

For when I "steal" a man's mind, I "steal" his personhood.

Thus Lavan can say as he confronts Jacob whom he suspects of duplicity, "... you have stolen my heart, by taking my daughters without my knowledge... you have stolen *me.*" (Genesis 33:26-27).

TAKING PEOPLE SERIOUSLY

It is very hard. The fortress of our self-esteem is constantly under attack. Not just from people who knock at our door to solicit our help, but from the neighbor who is too loud, the boss who is too overbearing, the co-worker who is too prying, the kids who mess up the driveway, and the fellow who calls in the middle of supper to sell long-life light bulbs, for whom nothing good at all can be said.

How do we talk? How do we act? How do we think? How do we feel? What will we tell our children about the dignity, the sheer grandeur, of being human?

And it matters. Oh how it matters! Our own failings will be multiplied ten-fold in them.

Here we are tested on a truly heroic scale. The battle of the pin-pricks. There is no hiding here. We will win or we will lose. Our children will be the medals of our glory or the marks of our shame. Living seriously is not easy.

לעולם ידור אדם בארץ ישראל אפילו
בעיר שרובה עכו"ם ואל ידור בחוצה
לארץ אפילו בעיר שרובה ישראל

One ought to choose to live in Eretz
Yisrael, even among non-Jews,
rather than to live outside Eretz
Yisrael, even among Jews. (Rambam, Melachim 5:12).

TAKING GALUTH SERIOUSLY

ETERNAL MISFITS

Our little book is written in English. It is meant
for those of us who have not yet gone home, who have
not yet been able or willing to put the advice of the
Rambam, with which we headed this chapter, into
practice.

Who are we? We are in many ways an assimi-
lated people. Not, God forbid, that we are lax in our
shemiras hamitzvos or in our commitment to Torah
study. But in the sense of a profound acculturation

within our host countries. This makes us comfortable with our surroundings and causes us to feel in some ways like strangers, even in Eretz Yisrael.

> ...It is virtually impossible even for a cloistered person not to be aware of the multicultural surroundings in...the Western World. The secular radio, the newspapers, even contact and conversations with people who are not religious or do not have a yeshiva background, must exercise influence. This can easily be seen, for example, in an American yeshiva student when he is put in a different setting, say in a yeshiva in Israel. His cultural attitudes from eating to reading are American, and his homeland in a deep sense is the USA. He feels at home there, whether because of baseball or business, food or newspapers or politics. In a sense he is an American who is an Orthodox Jew...[1]

Tucked away among all the comforts which cradle us in our host countries, there lurk some uncomfortable questions. These do not touch merely on whether we prefer a breakfast of cornflakes or *leben*. With that we can live. Rather, they address whole constellations of attitudes: the questions we ask, the news that engages our attention, the ideas which stimulate us, the traits we admire, the jokes at which we laugh, the goals which move us, our heroes and our villains, our fears and our dreams. Do we think and feel "Jewish", or are we some awful kind of hybrid upon which an alien cultural cluster makes a significant or even a controlling impact?

These are important questions.

Let us read a little Chumash:

> And you, I will scatter among the nations, I will unsheathe the sword after you; and your land will be desolate and your cities will be a ruin.

> Then the land will be appeased for its Shemitah during all the years of its desolation while you are in the land of your foes; then the land will rest and it will appease for all its [missed] Shemitos.

> ...

> The survivors among you -- I will bring weakness into their hearts in the land of their foes; the sound of a rustling leaf will pursue them, they will flee as one flees the sword, and they will fall but without a pursuer.

> ...

> You will become lost among the nations; the land of your foes will devour you.

Because of their iniquity, your remnant will disintegrate in the land of your foes; and because the iniquities of their forefathers are with them as well, they will disintegrate.

...

I too will behave toward them with casualness, and I will bring them into the land of their foes -- perhaps then their unfeeling heart will be humbled and then they will gain appeasement for their sin.

...

But despite all this, while they will be in the land of their foes, I will not have been revolted by them, nor will I have rejected them to obliterate them, to annul My covenant with them -- for I am HaShem their God (Leviticus 26:33-41).

The land of our foes! Five times in the course of eight verses!

It seems that however long fate compels us to stay there, however many generations will have been born there, for however long we will have been granted the privileges, and will have loyally shouldered the legitimate burdens of citizenship, we will never be more than aliens. The land of our exile will remain, must always remain, the land of our enemies.[2]

Enemies of what? Often enough of our very physical existence. We know the story. There is no need, in this context, to rehearse one more time what they have done to us. There is no need to identify the "they," no need to retell the horrors.

There are, however, more benign exiles. For the last several decades, we have found an uneasy welcome in the countries of the West, most particularly in America. True, there are occasional tremors. True, too, that there are dangers lurking. But, withal, we are not in physical danger. We are not loved but we are also not killed. Our religious freedoms are constitutionally guaranteed. Our Yeshivos are flourishing, our communal institutions are firmly anchored and richly endowed.

And still the Torah talks of אֶרֶץ אוֹיְבֵיהֶם. The threat is real, the more insidious because its form is more benign. What can we do to make sure that we feel *galuth* a little more? How can we make ourselves a little less comfortable?

AN ANCIENT TALE

There was once an island on which lived a group of women with truly beautiful voices. Sailors who manned the passing ships were so bewitched by their song, that they would direct their boats to the island only to founder on its treacherous shoals. There were three reactions to this problem among the captains of those ships. One forced all his men to stop up their ears with beeswax so that they were unable to hear. Another lashed the helmsman to the mast so that he was unable to alter course. The third provided music to his men that was so sweet that the song coming from the shore lost its allure.

I do not know whether Homer [the source for this cautionary tale] drew any of his wisdom from the prophets of the first Bais HaMikdash with whom he was contemporaneous, but it is certain that his story can serve as an appropriate mashal for the Torah's predictions concerning the final stages of exile, those immediately prior to the coming of Mashiach.

Let us listen to Rav Hutner. The time is a Seudas Purim, one of those moments when the inner fire that animated that great soul blazed to the surface. The place, his beloved Yeshiva where he knew that he would be understood.

This is what he said. After twenty long years of exile, Yaakov Avinu is finally returning to Eretz Yisrael. Eisav, sensing that his moment has come, prepares himself for the reckoning which, for once, must surely go his way.

We know the story and we know that this confrontation between the two brothers would, as our Sages understood it, presage every one of the subsequent encounters between their respective descendants. The blood, the tears, the sorrows and the triumphs of body and spirit which have punctuated our history, all inhered in those portentous moments.

Things did not work out as Eisav had hoped. The sword with which Yitzchak had blessed him proved impotent. Yaakov prevailed and will prevail.

But Eisav cannot, nor will he, give up. What will not yield to his open hate may yet succumb to his guile. Before he is finally relegated to the slag-heap of history, he will try one more thing. Perhaps a surface friendship will accomplish what overt enmity had not. He offers to have some of his men accompany Yaakov on his way.

A hand stretched out, a mask of good-will stretched thin over the hungry grimace of hate. What could be more innocent -- or more perniciously destructive!

"Let us travel and move on together. I will adjust my speed to your needs." "Let me assign to you some of the people who are with me" (Bereishis 33:11 and 15).

These were the last recorded words which Eisav ever spoke to Yaakov. They represent his game-plan for the final moments of the *galuth*. They hound us still. If we listen well, we hear them reverberating throughout the gilded cells which seem not to confine us, bouncing off the walls which seem to contain us not at all. They animate a culture which reaches out to smother us in its filthy embrace. They are the music in the message which wants to smash us on the rocks.

It is the last of the challenges which we will have to undergo. We have a number of options among which to chose. We may stop our ears with beeswax, tie ourselves to the masts or, more ideally, become attuned to a different, more alluring music.

TAKING GALUTH SERIOUSLY

Let us examine each of these three strategies.

Stopping the Ears: The pros and cons of engagement versus withdrawal touch upon every aspect of our lives. Where we work and where we play; how we travel and what we listen to; our shopping habits and the way we furnish our homes; what we wear and how we talk; and so on and on and on. We cannot even begin to think of touching on all of them.

In this essay, we will muse a little about only one aspect of this multi-faceted issue. The theories upon which we should try to build and develop the education of our children, given the realities which face us here in America.[3]

I admit to a personal quandary here. Do I shut out everything or do I listen selectively? Can we, as Rabbi Meir did in his time, savor the fruit while discarding the husk, or is the fusing so insidious, the tainting so pernicious, that we would do best to abandon the attempt?

I do not know. There are persuasive arguments and charismatic role models for both approaches. As I write these words, the tendency seems to be towards a greater withdrawal, a principled rejection of a culture which, with all its advantages, seems unable to get anything right. And that may be good. Nevertheless, it is not without its dangers.

Withdrawal is prompted by disapproval which, in turn, tends to spawn an attitude of supercilious, if occasionally benign, condescension. Jagged fissures inch their ugly way through communities which could and should function as a seamless whole. Gradations of values and attitudes which, grounded as they are in common assumptions and common goals, could simply have been accommodated within an overarching cohesion, become icons of a pernicious "in" which defines itself only in contrast to a demonized "out". I do not, of course, contend that solidarity ought to be purchased at any price[4]. Clearly, if the rejection of all or most of what our modern culture has to offer is necessary for the preservation of our values, we will have to live with that.

Nevertheless, it is not at all clear to me that such a virtually total repudiation is in fact necessary. Not all that has been and is being written is decadent. There are many religiously and ethically sensitive people who have much of significance to say. At the very least, they may offer pithy and insightful formulations, new bottles produced with verve and imagination, which may attractively contain the old wine of truth.[5]

Our thoughts here are in line with Maharatz Chayos' defense of Rambam's avid reading of the Greek and Arabic philosophers [Ateres Tzi, Tiferes LeMoshe, ch.3]. Rambam, so Maharatz Chayos claims, never used these books as the source of any of his rulings. Rather, the insights which he gleaned from them enabled him to understand the teachings of our Sages more profoundly.

Let us assume, however, that we deem the risks too great. We all know there is much which argues in favor of such an assessment.

Then, given that our decision is unlikely to be universally, or even generally accepted, we would need to adjust our educational agenda to that reality. We would need to teach our children that disagreement ought not to breed disparagement of people. That our preference to withdraw is a strategic move to protect our own, and not an actual or implied condemnation of those who are either less religiously sensitive than we, or who, conversely, feel more secure and therefore less threatened than we believe they ought to feel.

Tying ourselves to the mast: We must never dream another's dream; we must set our lives to the music which is ours alone. Our earlier ambivalence ought not to befuddle us here; our sense of the appropriate should be uncluttered by ambiguities. We must walk a lonely road -- because we are alone. We are different. We are chosen. We are holy.

Rabbi Chaim Segal, late Menahel of Mesivta Rabbeinu Chaim Berlin, reported that he once asked Rav Hutner what the central theme of our educational enterprise should be. Rav Hutner answered that, given the mindless blurring of differences which is the hallmark of modernity's headlong rush into conformity, our primary goal must be to strengthen our students' awareness of our chosenness. It is our fate and our calling to be different.

We need not, in the present context, belabor the sorry failures of the society in which we find ourselves. We all know, or should know, from what we must keep our distance. If we do not, or cannot, then rehearsing the various details here will not make much of a difference.

The question with which we as educators must grapple, is a different one. How do we reject the culture of our host countries while remaining good citizens? How do we isolate ourselves from huge segments of even our own people without falling prey to a mentality which tends to dehumanize those whose ideas we determinedly disavow and whose practices we abhor?

This is not an idle question. We are rarely understood, often disliked, sometimes even hated. This is a situation with which we should not be willing to make peace. To the extent that this is not our fault, it is not our concern. But there is much that we could do, and therefore much which, from the standpoint of *chinuch*, ought to engage our attention.

We are least nice when we are most threatened. Let us agree on this and draw some conclusions. We care about what others think of us. That is simply a fact. Not many of us feel comfortable putting on tallis and tefillin in a crowded plane.

Should we care? No and yes.

No, if by that we mean fostering self-confidence. We need not please every curious onlooker who might wrinkle his nose at what we do. When we act correctly, we owe explanations to no one at all.

Yes, if the alternative is disrespect and denigration. We ought never to forget that every human being, even if ignorant or prejudiced, is still a Tzelem Elokim who has claim on our consideration and understanding. We need not act as he would wish us to act, but we need to regard him as he would wish to be regarded. This balancing act is not an easy one, but if we are to retain our own humanity, it is a skill which we must learn and teach.

Let us then find in ourselves the courage to be different. Let us consciously, and with principled discipline, reject the habits and mores of the society in which we live; those that are tainted by corruption and even those which are neutral but simply superfluous, and therefore, irrelevant to our Jewish living. אל תשמח ישראל אל גיל כעמים, "Do not you, O Israel, find your enjoyment where the nations find theirs (Hosea 9:1)!" All, all, in our times, has been drained of innocence. Let us eschew what we cannot meaningfully assimilate.

Listening to a Different Tune: At the end of the day, there is really only one answer. Discipline, kedushah, service, these have a music of their own. The majestic resonance of their tone cuts right through to the heart. It can, if we let it, drown out the pathetic tinkle, trivialize to utter impotence the dross and the tinsel of even the best of what the world has to offer.

There really is no competition. But it has to be done right. The best music sounds bland and uninteresting when it is not performed with verve, with spirit, and above all, with intelligence.

חנוך לנער על פי דרכו, "Educate your son in accordance with his unique characteristics (Mishley 22:6)." We make facile assumptions at our peril. Assumptions that what worked well enough for ourselves will work equally well for our children. Assumptions that they must certainly share our tastes and predilections. Assumptions that the ideas that we found inspiring will fire their hearts also. It is just not so or, less radically, it is often not so.

We can occasionally create an environment that approximates an idealized earlier one, and hope that its ambiance will nurture an innocence more familiar from another era. It may work sometimes for some children.

But it is foolish to think that we can shut out the world indefinitely. The music is playing on the rocky island and sooner or later it will penetrate our most lovingly and thoughtfully erected defenses. Our lives will have to be set to music -- the ultimate weapon in the battle for our children's souls.[6]

ואהבת את ה' אלהיך...ובכל מאדך

Now you shall love HaShem your
God...with all your possessions.
(Devarim 6:5)

יש לך אדם שממונו חביב עליו מגופו

There are those whose money is
dearer to them than their own bod-
ies. (Berachos 61b)

TAKING MONEY SERIOUSLY

DESIRE BEGETS DESIRE

Do not lend against interest, for it gobbles
up the borrower's wealth. Do not bloat
yourself at his expense when you lend him
food (Vayikra 25:17).

This is a loose translation of the verse that prohib-
its taking interest from a fellow Jew. It is not a particu-

larly good translation; it is really more of a paraphrase. But it does try to capture the Torah's disgust at the usurer. נשך, to bite, conjures up the picture of the snapping, rending predator. מרבית, bloat[1], describes the gloating money-bags who fattens himself on someone's hunger pangs.

What is wrong with taking interest? All of us can understand why we ought not to take advantage of our fellow's misery by lending him against unconscionably high rates. That is usury and would be condemned in any enlightened society. But what is wrong with charging a reasonable amount for the use of our resources? Why can we, without raising anyone's eyebrows, rent out our homes, our cars or our tools, but not our money? What underlies the difference?

The Torah's term for money is כסף [kesef]. The word derives from the root כסף [kosof], to crave. Every other object in the world has intrinsic value. It is what it is and needs nothing external to give it validity and standing. Only money has its significance defined solely in terms of what it can buy. Postulate an empty store and you may as well throw your wealth to the winds. Money can fulfill desires, or it can do nothing at all. At the end of the day it is no more and no less than a solid chunk of wanting. It is desire made tangible.

Interest which is nothing more than money begetting money, is ultimately craving begetting craving. This the Torah refuses to sanction. Certainly there is no intention to crimp the normal, and in itself legitimate, development of commerce. Obviously, people must be able to raise cash and where capital is otherwise simply not attainable, the mechanism that makes the היתר עיסקא possible is in place.[2] But not lending for lending's sake. Not a prostitution of the faculty for infinite longing with which God has endowed us. For a prostitution it would be. Let us explain.

Why, asks R' Tzadok HaKohen of Lublin, is man, who in his physiology is so similar to the animal world, so different from the animals when it comes to over-indulging? Animals are not as a rule sybarites. They mate as the instinct to propagate the species demands; they sleep as their body craves rest; they hunt and feed as their need for food makes itself felt. There is no ambition beyond this.

How different we are! How fiercely do our urges drive us! Why are just we, in all of God's wondrous world, so prone to excess? Because, R' Tzadok teaches, we are not animals. Our agenda goes beyond the filling of our physical needs, the assuaging of our hunger pangs, the perpetuation of our kind. David sang of a soul thirsting for You, of flesh pining for You (Tehilim 63:2). To long for the ever unattainable, the absolute beyond, that requires a faculty for infinite desire. There is never to be sufficiency, never absolute fulfillment.

There is always more that we want. And more. And more. And then some more. And when we degrade this faculty by permitting it to focus upon the physical, we are prostituting the most precious of the gifts with which God has endowed us.

And this the Torah will not tolerate. Let desire not beget desire. Let money not breed money. There are better ways to use the boundless longings that animate our souls.[3]

A CELESTIAL ACCOUNTING SYSTEM

There is much that we need to teach our children about prudent money management. We shall fail unless we first teach ourselves.

Let us think a little about our own budget. We tend to buy what we can afford. In the relaxed and understanding society in which we live, it seems legitimate to do so. Advertisers know us well and come at us from every direction by every means. We, so they tell us, deserve the best, and most of us tend to agree heartily. As long as we do not hurt anyone, as long as our resources bear up, why not?

But the Torah has different ideas. Chovos Ha-Levavos, in his classic discussion of *bitachon*, maintains that people are mistaken when they believe that their money is to be regarded as unreservedly and legitimately available for the gratification of their every want, their every perceived need. Property, he asserts, is to be viewed as consisting of three categories. The first is that which God grants us for the provision of our own needs. The second is that which we receive in order to conscientiously and adequately fulfill our family responsibilities. So far so good.

There is, however, a third category. This is money that God deposits in our account, so to speak, but which He does not necessarily intend for the assuaging of our own hungers. It may well be, so he asserts pungently, that it is given to whom it is given so that he might preserve it for his wife's next husband.[4]

The implications of this proposition are shattering. Were a person to use this portion of his wealth for his own gratification, he would do so illegitimately. He would be drawing on funds to which he has no right[5] and would, so one supposes on the basis of many well-known midrashim, be using up capital from his portion in the World-to-Come.[6]

Now comes the problem. How, if we accept this premise, are we to know what is what? When can we draw upon our resources with a clear conscience, and when must we fear that our spending is illicit?

In the absence of some celestial bank statement that spells out the precise size of each allocation, we have no choice but to rely upon our own judgment. Good enough. But on what basis can we decide?

Clearly there is only one way. If we live as we must suppose that God would have us live, frugally and modestly, we are entitled to assume that we are not overstepping any bounds. God is not seeking to entrap us.

If, however, we indulge in more than we can reasonably assume is our due, then we are in real danger of making some dreadful mistakes. We may discover when it is too late to do anything about it, that we have drawn upon funds that were morally, if not legally, out of bounds. There will be less for us in Olam HaBa. We will have traded the eternal for the transient, the truly satisfying for the brittle junk of the cereal box teaser.

Things look differently from such a perspective. It transpires that the test against which we must measure our acquisitions is not whether we can afford them, but whether we deserve them. Before we indulge in the model year for which we yearn, the imposing home of our dreams or the designer suit which tickles our vanity, we would need to ask some very probing questions. Few will have the confidence to assert that their desires are necessarily congruent with the dispositions which God has made for supplying them with their legitimate needs.

Thus we must learn to do with less than we might want. The healthy bottom line of our bank statement tells us nothing at all. We must consult our conscience, not our estate planner. We must live differently, and seriously.

If we make a success of our own lives, we may at least hope that our children will become efficient and conscientious money managers.

רבי טרפון אומר: היום קצר והמלאכה
מרובה והפועלים עצלים והשכר הרבה
ובעל הבית דוחק.

Rabbi Tarfon taught: The day is
short but there is much work to be
done. The workers are lazy though
there is much to be gained. The
owner is insistent. (Avos 2:15)

TAKING TIME SERIOUSLY

A PILE OF NUTS

Maseches Avos is the repository of all those
fundamental ideas that animated the lives of our great
teachers. We will not expect to find there the trite, the
merely pithy or the obvious.

What, then, is Rabbi Tarfon really saying? Is it not
self-evident that life is all too short, that we must jeal-
ously husband each unforgiving minute, and that the
vast complexities of the Torah could fill many lifetimes
many times over?

We would like to postulate that, perhaps, in Rabbi Tarfon's mouth, addressed to Rabbi Tarfon's students, these words had a very special meaning.

Let us examine the first part of the statement:

היום קצר - והמלאכה מרובה

THE DAY IS SHORT
BUT THERE IS MUCH WORK TO DO.

Gittin 67a reports that the Tanna Issi ben Yehudah was able to describe the unique qualities of some of the Sages of his age, often by means of a pithy and finely crafted metaphor. For the great Rabbi Tarfon, he thought that comparison to a pile of nuts would serve well. It expressed graphically how this great scholar approached his studies. When he was asked a question concerning, let us say, a mishnah, he would not be satisfied with an answer that dealt only with the immediate context. The principle that he enunciated would have to be borne out in scriptural, midrashic and aggadic sources too. Much as one nut withdrawn from a pile brings all the others tumbling down around it, the initial reference would generate an avalanche of unsuspected contexts in which the given proposition was shown to be relevant.

Rabbi Tarfon, then, saw unity among the many seemingly discrete levels of Torah. An assertion that could be validated only within its own particular setting,

was, in his mind, inadequate. Much more work needed
to be done; many other fields probed and tested for
support or contradiction.

   This, perhaps, is what he meant when he asserted
that והמלאכה מרובה, there is much work to be done --
too much for the ordinary day. The facile acceptance of
the immediately attractive, the context-friendly but
shallow, answer, does not require an inordinate amount
of time. We all know that it can be handled. But the
conscientious exploration of strange areas, of seemingly
unrelated sources -- that is another matter. The day is all
too short for that.[1]

****

   We now turn to the second part of Rabbi Tarfon's
teaching.

והפועלים עצלים - והשכר הרבה
THE WORKERS ARE LAZY
THOUGH THERE IS MUCH TO BE GAINED.[2]

   The "workers" are, of course, Every Man in relation
to the obligations defined in the earlier phrase under the
rubric, והמלאכה מרובה. But what does Rabbi Tarfon
want to convey with this teaching? He offers an observa-
tion, not an exhortation.

   What are we to make of this?

We will do well to examine this issue in the light
of Mesilas Yesharim's discussion of זריזות, the ebullient,
energetic pursuit of duty (ch. 6):

> Clearly man's nature tends towards
> the lethargic, since physicality by its very
> essence is gross. Because of this we shy
> away from effort and labor.
>
> One who really wants to serve God,
> would have to battle and ultimately over-
> power his own nature; summoning both
> strength and energetic enthusiasm to the
> task at hand.
>
> Success would, without any doubt,
> elude one who allows himself to succumb
> to his natural grossness...

Mesillas Yesharim goes on to describe how our
natural tendency towards languor and lassitude can, and
ultimately will, enfeeble our learning. Insufficient effort
leads to imperfect understanding which, in turn, leads to
misguided application; and ultimately, by way of the determination to defend the indefensible, to an entire
edifice of falsehood and deception.

Rabbi Tarfon makes this very point. Our propensity towards inertia is a given. Even though "there is
much to be gained," even though there is sheer intellectual exhilaration in tracing propositions to their every

manifestation, in hunting down every last area in which they might have relevance, it is still not enough. Unless we fight our unfortunate indolence fiercely, not every last nut will come tumbling down.

It is only the awareness that, "...the owner is insistent" that will force us into harness. This is the legacy which Rabbi Tarfon, the "pile of nuts", wanted to leave to posterity.

RABBI TARFON WAS TALKING TO US -- NOT ONLY TO OUR CHILDREN

I know two stories. Here is the first.

A man was making a call from a pay-phone. After he hung up, the operator came on the line to tell him to put in another quarter. The man was upset. Why make such a fuss over such a negligible amount of money? The operator answered, "The fuss I am making is about the same quarter which you are even now trying to salvage with such tenacity."

We tend to be more forgiving of ourselves than we are of our children. That will not work. It is the same quarter. It is the same quarter of an hour. If it means nothing to us, our children will pay it short shrift. We deceive ourselves at our own and our children's peril.

How do we translate Rabbi Tarfon's lofty aspirations into our own more pedestrian abilities?

Rabbi Moshe Sternbuch, in Mo'adim UZemanim, vol 2, p141, has some interesting thoughts. Megilah 3a teaches that on Purim, we must interrupt our learning in order to listen to the Megilah being read. But, commentators ask, why is listening to the Megilah viewed as an interruption of Torah study? It is a part of the T'NaCh and as a *bona fide* biblical book ought to qualify as Torah study in its own right.

Not at all, says Rabbi Sternbuch. Time can be squandered in destructive fashion vertically as well as wasted horizontally. It is not only unfilled minutes or hours which count as a dead loss, but also superficial scanning which leaves lodes of potential meaning unmined, and ideas which matter, undeveloped. The Megilah is Torah, but listening to it is not <u>learning</u> Torah.

Nor does any learning which does not engage the creative energy of which we are capable[3] qualify as a constructive use of time.[4] We cannot, if we expect our visit to be rewarding, simply cruise through a *sugya* paying courtesy calls at points of interest but being unwilling to invest commitment amid the sweat and jostle of the local bazaars. We must tumble our own pile of nuts,

If we want to make real *masmidim* of our children, we must show them the way.

It is not so easy to be a good learner or a good parent.

Here is the second story. A father was concerned about his son's attitude towards learning. The boy never seemed to want to open the gemara at home. The father tried everything in the book. He offered inducements and hired private Rebbis. Nothing helped. The boy was simply not interested.

The last in a long line of frustrated Rebbis finally decided to have a talk with the boy. How could he be so uncaring in the light of his father's many and loving efforts? Could he not try a little harder to show his appreciation?

The boy, as children will do, told the truth. "If Dad thinks that learning is so important, how come he never cracks a sefer?"

The father took the rebuke to heart and began a serious seder. Thereafter he had no more problems with his son.

The day is short and there is indeed much work to be done. In the context of our discussion, we may say that there is also much reward to be garnered. Beyond the satisfaction of really understanding the material that we are studying, there is the untold joy of seeing our children blossoming. Things do not get much better than that.

כבד את ה' מהונך -- ממה שחננך

Honor God with the gifts with
which He has endowed you!
(Pesikta d'Rav Kahana, based on
Mishley 3:9)

TAKING WORK AND PLAY SERIOUSLY

WE ARE WHAT WE ARE

We paraphrase the full passage from which we
took the small quotation that we placed at the head of
this chapter.

Honor God with the gifts with which
He has endowed you!
If, for example, you have a pleasant
voice, use it to lead the congregation in
prayer. Rabbi Elazar ben Aroch had a
nephew who sang well. He urged him to
serve as chazan. That would be his way of

honoring God with that with which he had been gifted.

There is also Naboth who had a pleasant voice and would often go up to Jerusalem to perform. People would flock to hear him. One day he decided not to go and as a result many people did not visit the Temple that day. As punishment he fell prey to Jezebel's scheming and was killed.

Of what was he guilty? Of not using the talent which God had granted him. (See Yalkut Shimoni, I Kings 221).

We have two implications here: Talents are for using; they are a mark of grace, a road sign that points us in the direction which God would have us follow. Allow them to atrophy and you have spurned God's favor. Develop them and you may be reasonably certain that you are on the right path. They are wasted, however, unless they are used for God's greater glory. God's gifts come wrapped in purpose.

Chovos HaLevavos [Shaar HaBitachon, Chapter 3, Hakdamah 5] gives us an inkling of his ideas on the subject. In discussing how one might determine the field of endeavor particularly suited to him, he writes: "For every man has an instinctive liking for certain kinds of work or business. It is comparable to the cat's instinct for catching mice...the heron's for catching fish...where each living creature is endowed with those physical attributes which are appropriate to its means of obtaining food...In this same way each person's individual nature is attuned to the kind of activity which God has in mind for him."

It is the same thought in different words. Awareness of particular gifts will deny us some of the comforts of conformity. But we must dare to be different because we are different.[1] Each of our particular mix of quirks, feelings and dreams is as unique as our features. Bland uniformity must not be tolerated. It squelches the spark, dulls the cutting edge of creativity, and impugns the צלם אלהים, the God-like singularity with which we have been irrevocably stamped.[2]

TO EACH HIS OWN

Build a house; plant a vineyard; become betrothed to a woman. What have you done? You have embarked upon a venture that frees you from fighting in certain of Israel's wars.

When an army is to be mustered, all who fall within any of these categories are sent home before the fighting begins. So too is one who is afraid.

For this last one, however, the Torah ascribes a reason. Fear is catching; it debilitates, it saps courage, corrodes the optimism and determination that are the stuff from which victory is fashioned. Better to throw out the one bad apple before the entire pile rots away.

But what of the other three? Why worry about their life more than that of anybody else? Rashi offers an explanation. The death of these, at the threshold of their great adventures, would cause the greater עגמת נפש, the greater sorrow.

Perhaps, if we permit ourselves a little *drush* license, another approach is possible.

Let us analyze the implications. By what right does government draft people into the army? What justifies the state in demanding that its citizens disrupt, and often lose their lives, give up their plans and dreams, leave their children without guidance, their wives without the warmth and loving presence of their husbands?

Clearly, the underlying principle is that communal need overrides any individual's right to decide what he wants to do with his life. חייך קודמין, the preeminent obligation to preserve one's own life before caring for that of any other, is inapplicable in time of war. The safety of the community comes first.[3]

But what if military service is not the most significant contribution that a given person can make to his people? What if the community were better served by sparing him the draft in order to enable him to give that which is uniquely in his power to bestow?

Then surely the army would have to forgo its claims. There are greater things in store for this man, greater services that he can render to his people. This may be the justification for the release from service for the three cat-egories which we are examining.

As a community, we ought not to deny ourselves the lessons which can be gleaned from the unique constellation of attitudes, talents and ideas which this particular man can summon as he enters his newly built house, harvests his freshly planted vineyard or marries his betrothed.

The "house" is the base from which we interact with society as good, or not such good, neighbors and citizens. The "vineyard" generates our livelihood and propels us into the marketplace where we are subject to the acid-test of ambition and competition, a place where we can sow strife and ruin if we allow ourselves to be driven by our base longings, or secure eternity by an ethical stance born of consideration and love. And our wife is our home. A home where we can break lives with autocratic, overbearing selfishness, or fashion worlds out of a love of God that translates into the stuff of which good spouses, parents and children are made.

The Torah teaches us that a man who has embarked upon any of these ventures should not be interrupted before we have had the chance to savor his unique contribution. He has much to give his people as a soldier bearing arms, but he can contribute infinitely more by building his peerless world and sharing with all of us those insights and dispositions that can never be duplicated by another.

We are what we are. We must work with what we have. We can, indeed we must, make of our particular lives that which only we can make of them.

A TIME TO PLAY

It is not easy to find sources in our literature that deal with playing in the sense that we, in our society, understand it. We have borrowed our heading, *A Time To Play,* from Koheles 3:4, in the full knowledge that it is doubtful that this is really the meaning of the phrase as the megillah uses it. Play, after all, belongs very specifically to the context of our affluent society. Only quite recently have people had the time and wealth to indulge in life's less serious pursuits. Earlier generations simply did not have that luxury.

Is there, then, anywhere that we can turn? We have Rambam in the Shmoneh Perakim who -- loosely rendered -- writes as follows: [While in general we should never indulge ourselves, but should rather choose that which is healthful over that which is simply enjoyable] there are occasions when pleasure itself may be therapeutic. Thus, when feeling depressed, we can revive our spirits with pleasant music, a stroll in the garden, or perhaps by contemplating beautiful buildings or communing with art. [Once mental health is restored, we can go back to the main concern of our existence. Robust in mind and body, we are to pursue the knowledge of God to the extent that we are capable.][4]

This is not exactly what we are looking for, but it is close enough for our purposes.

Everybody needs an occasional break. Berachos 28a tells that when R' Zeira was simply too exhausted to continue learning, he would sit at the entrance of the Bais HaMidrash so that he could rise in a show of respect to the scholars who were entering or leaving. If for the moment he was unable to learn, he would at least demonstrate his love for Torah by doing what he could.

R' Zeira was no ordinary person. He was so serious that no smile ever crossed his face [Nidah 23a] nor would he ever waste even a moment of his precious time [Megillah 28a]. Such a man can never serve as a natural paradigm for those of us who cannot even remotely approach his greatness. There is, nonetheless, something that this gemara can teach us about acceptable forms of adult recreation.

How are we to understand R' Zeira's action?

In the synthesis that is yielded by the disparate elements, *avdut* [service required of us] and *nedivut* [service rendered out of love rather than from any obligation], these two are not present in equal amounts at all times. Occasionally, the *ol* [yoke]-factor is dominant, while *nedivut* plays the more muted role. It serves as an accompanist: harmonizing, softening, sweetening and wearing away the hard abrasive edges of servitude. At other times, *nedivut* holds center stage. These are moments in which being preponderates over doing, in which the *ol*-factor is no more than the disciplining hand upon the reins, the assurance that love, by its very nature antagonistic to restraint, will not exceed the bounds of propriety.[5]

When R' Zeira learned, it was the driving *ol* that animated and contoured his efforts. At rest, he allowed *nedivut* to come to the fore. Surely there was no specific obligation to choose to sit just where the students would be passing. The obligation to show respect for Talmidei Chachamim by standing up for them does not oblige us to seek them out for this purpose. But love knows no bounds and R' Zeira was a man in love. If he could not himself study, he would at least show his respect for those students who could.

This interpretation could yield a satisfying paradigm for adult play. It is a form of spending time during which it is appropriate to adjust amounts and proportions in the *avdut-nedivut* polarity within our Jewish make-up. As R' Zeira did before us, we need to find outlets in which we are able to *be* rather than to *do*, in which our love and respect for what we do at other times can come to the fore.

WHAT ABOUT THE KIDS?

Children, of course, are different. There is evidence, sparse but adequate, of tolerant attitudes towards their playful inclinations. Perhaps -- who can know -- games were even encouraged. Thus, we let children run and jump on Shabbos even though such behavior is not really consistent with the spirit of the day (Orach Chaim 302); and even on Yom Kippur we permit them to play with nuts (Orach Chaim 611), rolling them and banging them together for sound (Mishna Berura 338:18).[6]

These are just a couple of examples. It seems to me that it is not even necessary to belabor the point. "The ways of the Torah are ways of pleasantness," and children clearly need to play[7]. But they do not need to play computer games.

It is obvious that we want activities which are supportive of, or at the very least, not antithetical to, values which are important to us. The computer's animated dream-worlds with their compelling images, exciting plots and raucous music, often fail badly in this regard. They seduce our children along paths which lead far far away from our Shabbos tables and our Seder, our Tish'ah Be'Av and our Succah, our *Bein Adam Le-Chaveiro* and our abhorrence of the mean, the violent, the crass and the banal.

Look at a picture of the Chafetz Chaim which may be gracing your wall as it does in so many Jewish homes.

Then, if you can bear to, look at the screen. Which do you want?[8]

There is also another consideration. When a child plays, it is good; when an adult plays, it is sad. We ought to encourage children to play those games which are appropriate to their age and interests, and which will fall away naturally as maturity makes them more and more irrelevant. In our benighted age, when children, paradoxically enough, age long before their times, adults wallow in puerility into their dotage. If you doubt this, think of the billions of glassy eyes glued helplessly and hopelessly to the televisions. Or walk down the aisle in a plane or on a train and observe what many people are doing with their lap-tops. Computer games are the wrong choice. They are hard to give up and for all their palm-held lightness and convenience, become heavy albatrosses to be dragged wearily through life.

A little pride goes a long way. We were saved from Egypt because we clung tenaciously to our own names, language and culture. We and our children do not have to become so much cannon fodder for the manic marksmen who target us in order to peddle their inanities from the cyber world[9]

צמאה לך נפשי כמה לך בשרי
בארץ ציה ועיף בלי מים.

My soul thirsts for You, my
flesh yearns for You; in a
parched land without water.
(Tehillim 63:2)

TAKING PRAYER SERIOUSLY

THE FURTHER WE ARE THE CLOSER WE ARE

Let us learn something about prayer.

...לבני קרח
כאיל תערג על אפיקי מים כן נפשי תערג אליך אלהים
צמאה נפשי לאלהים לאל חי

...Composed by the sons of Korach:
My soul longs for You O God, as the
parched deer pines for the gushing waters.
My soul thirsts for God,
the living God. (Tehillim 42:2-3)

An arid desert. A fainting deer crazed by thirst. Visions of a sparkling spring. A scream. That is prayer.

לבני קרח... How did Korach's children understand the art of prayer so well? Let us listen to Rashi: [Korach's sons were] Asir, Elkanah and Eviasaph. They had once been part of Korach's cabal in his rebellion against Moshe. When they realized the enormity of what was happening, they parted company with him. When the earth opened its maw to swallow the insurgents, it provided a secure platform for these three within the pit...It was from there that they composed their songs of adoration...

A narrow platform teetering over the edge of a bottomless abyss. The intersection between unrelieved despair and unquenchable hope provides the impetus for man to meet his God.

We all must occasionally make our way through our own Valley of Despondency. It is up to us to experience our sense of distance so clearly that God's closeness thrusts itself upon our consciousness as the only possible elixir of life. By means of such experiences does He help us to draw the poetry of prayer from our hearts.

SCALING HEIGHTS AND BRIDGING CHASMS

Abba Binyamin taught: Ideally prayer should take place in the synagogue [rather than in the home or some other place][1]. For it is written [in the inaugural prayer which Solomon offered at the dedication of his Temple], ...לשמוע אל הרנה, ואל התפלה [that God might] hearken to the רנה and the תפלה [which he offered up that day.] [I Kings 8:28]. [The juxtaposition of תפלה to רנה yields:] במקום רנה שם תהא תפלה. Prayer is to be undertaken specifically at locations which are devoted to רנה [and that is the synagogue] [Berachos 6a].

We have left רנה untranslated, the better to facilitate an analysis of this passage.

תפלה is of course prayer. רנה [from רנן, to give a ringing cry] can be used both for calls of exultation [Yirmiyahu 31:6, parallel to צהלה] and for cries of distress [Eichah 2:19].

In what sense, then, is the synagogue described as a location devoted to רנה? Rashi offers the following: The synagogue is the place where the community sings sweet songs of praise [to God]. רנה, then, in this context is used for devotional song, the recitation of psalms.

But we are not told why just this use, to which the synagogue is often put, makes it the ideal forum for תפלה.[2]

Gra to Mishley 1:20 offers a different explanation, one which places this gemara squarely within the ambit

of our earlier discussion. We found that it is an awareness of distance and alienation which ideally summons
us to prayer. Gra teaches that it is in the synagogue, of all
places, that such a feeling is best nurtured.

How so? The Mishley text reads as follows:
חכמות בחוץ תרנה, ברחובות תתן קולה, בראש המיות תקרא,
בפתחי שערים אמריה תאמר. Wisdom is depicted as
moving slowly from outside the town towards its center,
always, along the way, calling out for attention. The
sound grows from the faint, undifferentiated רנה, which
can only just be heard from far away [בחוץ תרנה], until it
progresses, always louder, always clearer, through the
stages of, first, קריאה and then נתינת קול and finally
אמירה. This last, taking place at the very gates of the
homes, can be fully understood. In this hierarchy of
sound, רנה is the least distinct. It is wisdom at its most
distant.

Why is the synagogue a מקום רנה, a place where
wisdom seems to be so very far away? Because, Gra
explains, it was the custom to have the little children,
aleph beis scholars, take their first uncertain steps in
Torah learning there. Shul is where wisdom is still at
arm's length and nothing much is really understood[3]. It
is the ultimate "בחוץ" of Torah.

And it is there, and only there, that we ought to
pray! In our petitions, we are to join the little ones
clamoring with their unformed minds to beat back the
barriers of ignorance. We too need to battle, need to

scale heights and bridge chasms. We and they are on the outside. We and they must be determined to penetrate to the innermost chambers.

COUNTING FOOTSTEPS

We walk to Shul and we go into a Succah. Ostensibly these are similar acts, but halachically they are very different from one another. Let us analyze this proposition.

Sotah 22a tells of a woman who had a synagogue in her neighborhood, but would, nevertheless, always attend one which was further away. She explained that by walking the extra distance she would merit שכר פסיעות, a reward for every step that she took. Midrash Rabba [Margalioth] at Devarim 7:2 tells of God "counting" our steps as we walk to Shul.

Now Maharal [Nesivos Olam, Nesiv haAvodah 5] points out that no such concept would apply when walking, let us say, to a Succah, or indeed to any other mitzvah. No merit at all would attach to choosing a Succah which was further away, no steps would be counted. Only convenience will determine which one is to be used.

Why is going to Shul different? Because, says Maharal, prayer in the synagogue is a matter of eliminating distance, of cleaving to the Divine Presence which is ensconced there. Walking to a Succah is simply the means of getting where you need to go and is in no sense a part of the fulfillment of the *mitzvah*. Walking to Shul is itself one aspect of the expression of devotion which is the essence of prayer. The very first step which we take on our way to Shul sets in motion a mighty continuum of ever-growing intimacy which finds its culmination in that heady moment when we find ourselves [or, more correctly, lose ourselves] in actual communion with God.[4]

****

Davening is not easy. We all know this and we also know our pitiful failings, our disgraceful lack of concentration. Its very difficulty makes it a significant *chinuch* challenge, both to our own development as serious Jews and to how well we do in educating our children towards a life of respectable prayer. If during the *shemoneh esrei,* we find our minds wandering every which way instead of focusing upon Him before Whom we are standing and hungering, then we must wonder whether our parents did well enough in teaching us how to go about the job.

We ourselves are now the parents who can make or break our children. What a dreadful responsibility!

Strangely enough, we tend to take a cavalier attitude towards even simple halachic directives which could, at the very least, ease our heavy burden. In our short essay, we have touched on two of these: the preference of the halachah that we go to Shul in order to pray; and that, given a choice, we should go to a further rather than a closer location.

Now there are few people who, given a lengthy walk to synagogue, would not take advantage of an ad hoc *minyan* organized in the neighborhood. Inescapably, we give our children the impression that the easy way is the better way and that it all does not matter very much.

Just imagine if instead of choosing convenience, we would by-pass the local option and take the long road to Shul. To parry the inevitable questions, we could invoke the ideas adumbrated above. We could tell our children how each step is precious -- counted by God -- as it brings us ever closer to the high moment when we can actually stand in His presence and pour out our hearts to Him. We could imbue them with the beginnings of a sense of awe and anticipation and, who knows, perhaps make serious *daveners* out of them[5].

Oh well, for most of us I suspect all this will remain a dream. Some dreams, however, are worth dreaming. And, as long as we are dreaming, let us go all the way and imagine ourselves feeling about prayer as the great Kuzari would have us feel:

>...Thus that he will not pray by rote
>as though he were a myna bird or a parrot,

but utter each word with thought and feeling.

Thus that the time of prayer will become the central energizing force of his life as also the fruit of his living. That all other activities become significant only to the extent that they lead to these moments ...

That the times set aside for prayer should be for his soul what mealtimes are for his body. Prayer sustaining his spiritual life as food sustains his physical life. That as the blessing of one prayer session begins to weaken he should hunger for the next one as surely as he hungers for the evening meal as the energy provided by breakfast begins to wear off... [Kuzari 3:5]

I know it is only a dream. But...

...ומה תקות הנברא אם לא ישים עמל
נפשו ועיקר עסקו בדברים שנברא בעבורם
[רבינו יונה, שערי תשובה ג:יז]

[Man owes his existence to God.] What hope for him if he forgets this truth and fails to focus his efforts upon those purposes for which he was created? [Rabbeinu Yonah, Shaarey Teshuvah 3:17]

THE SUM OF THE MATTER WHEN ALL HAS BEEN CONSIDERED[1]

AT THE SOUTH POLE

The United States maintains the Amundsen-Scott Research Station at the South Pole. The low humidity creates ideal conditions for astronomers to have a clear window on the universe and what the telescopes can do there they cannot duplicate anywhere else.

Life is not easy. Winter in the Antarctic means six dreary months of total darkness -- twenty-four hours a day -- with temperatures averaging 60 degrees below zero. Dips into minus three digits are not uncommon.

So why live there? For the committed scientist, the question is a non-starter. The tantalizing mysteries of space exert their own magnetism. He goes where the answers are. The numbing cold, the rugged, lonesome life, is a small price to pay for the speck of insight that he can pluck out of infinity. For that, it makes sense to suffer.

And for a very similar reason, God sends our נשמות, our souls, down to this world. It is cold down here, and rugged, and lonesome. For the princess whose natural environment is the palace, it is no better than the miserable hovel of a destitute peasant[2]. But there is work to be done here, very very important work, and that makes it all worth-while[3]. Provided that we use our time wisely.

It is inconceivable that an astronomer at the Pole would forego a particularly advantageous moment for viewing the sky because he just happens to be curled up comfortably reading a Reader's Digest. He has sacrificed too much, gone through too much, to treat opportunity in so cavalier a fashion. It ought to be equally inconceivable for us to waste any time at all. The princess in the peasant's hut must ask herself very thoughtfully why she is there. If she is convinced that she came for a purpose, she would do well to take that purpose seriously.

There is a great deal at stake.

****

IN BENEI BERAK

I recall a small room in Benei Berak. It is evening and Shabbos is slowly ebbing away. It is summer and the heat is merciless. People are crushed together and overflowing into the tiny hallway. They squeeze into each other so that the center of the room is left free. A space, a shtender and an old man, frail and bent. That is all. A barely audible voice thundering in the hearts of the listeners. The Mashgiach[4] in the last months of his life, too weak to speak in the huge Bais haMidrash, is giving the Shabbos evening Schmuss[5].

It is getting darker outside, but this is the Chazon Ish's Benei Berak and so no electricity, generated as it is by Jewish labor, is allowed to offend the sanctity of Shabbos. We can see, but only just. And what we see is a face which none of us will ever forget. There is no smile there, no drama, none of the qualities that scream charisma in our tinsel world. It is an eloquent face. It speaks of desperate longing, of dreadful fear of failure and of passionate love. It is, in the end, no more than a window into an unblemished soul scoured bright in myriad battles, reflecting the victories that are the trophies of a life earnestly lived in the presence of God.

No words will ever capture that face. Those who saw it need none; those who never saw it, well, they just did not. Nothing will ever make up for that loss.

But let us listen to what the Mashgiach is saying. On the particular evening in question, he is concentrating on a text in the third Shaar of Rabbeinu Yonah's Shaarey Teshuvah. He adds nothing at all to what is written there. His message lies in the repetition again and again and yet again of the same words and the same words, and yet again the same words, until by the force of their eloquence and the fire of his conviction they become seared on everyone's heart.

Here is his text:

...ובעבור המעלות האלה נברא האדם,...ומה תקות הנברא אם לא ישים עמל נפשו ועיקר עסקו בדברים שנברא בעבורם.

A little background before we translate. In this same section Rabbeinu Yonah had provided a list of מעלות, supreme qualities that define Jewish aspirations. They are: The quality of taking control of one's life [מעלת הבחירה][6]; the quality of Torah study [מעלת תלמוד תורה]; the quality of fashioning one's life so that he walks in God's ways [מעלת לכת בדרכי ה']; the quality of thinking deeply about God's greatness [מעלת התבונן בגדלות ה'] ; the quality of being constantly and deeply aware of God's kindness [מעלת זכרון חסדי ה' והתבונן בהם]; the quality of sanctity [מעלת הקדושה]; the quality of service [מעלת העבודה]; the quality of awe [מעלת היראה]; the quality of love [מעלת האהבה]; and the quality of cleaving to God [מעלת הדבקות].

The concluding sentence of the paragraph in which these qualities are listed is the one that we have quoted. Herewith a loose translation, really more of a paraphrase:

Only the possibility for us to aspire to these supreme qualities, nothing else, can explain why God would have created us...Can we then conceive of man who owes his entire existence to God, doing anything else but focusing his best efforts towards the fulfillment of the very purpose for which he was created? Can there be any hope for him if he ignores this duty?

The Mashgiach cannot tear himself away. ומה תקוה...ומה תקוה...ומה תקוה. The futility of the wasted life, the sheer sorrow and pity of the unfulfilled potential, the unused opportunity fills his being with overwhelming compassion. He begs, he cajoles he entreats us to understand. Don't just hear the words and then leave them behind. There is no hope at all, there really isn't, for all of us, for you and for you and for you, but most of all for me, if I, if you, if all of us cannot learn to live life seriously.

At the end of the day, that is the lesson that we must leave with our children. But then, we must first learn it ourselves, and learn it well.

ENDNOTES

SOME REFLECTIONS ABOUT THE REFLECTIONS

1. From, ed. Moshe Sokol, *Rabbinic Authority and Personal Autonomy*, Jason Aronson Inc. New Jersey.

2. Reference is to Devarim 12:17 where the Torah forbids the eating of certain things under given circumstances. Instead of the expected "You **may** not..." we have, "You **can** not ..." To this, Rashi brings the midrash: Rabbi Yehoshua ben Korchah taught: You are **able** to, but you are not permitted. The sense is that God's awesome presence should be so real to us that we should simply not have sufficient control of our limbs to do that which He forbids.

    In this connection, it is appropriate to consider Bereishis Rabba 67:3. There R' Levi teaches: Man is endowed with two groups of three servants each: His eyes, his nose and his ears, his hands, legs and mouth. He cannot control the first three [that is, if his eyes are open he cannot avoid seeing, if his ears are unstopped he cannot avoid hearing, if his nasal passages are unclogged he cannot avoid smelling.] But he can control the second group [that is he need not move his hands or his feet unless he wishes to; he need not speak unless he decides that that is what he wants to do.] If he merits it, those which he controls **will also be removed from his control**.

    The idea is once more the same. We do not crave absolute freedom but absolute submission.

3. The sense here is that the Exodus did not grant us freedom in the conventional sense, but rather changed our vassal state from being Pharaoh's servants to being servants of God.

4. What is worrying about "making one's own decisions" is the sense that there are absolutely no objective standards.

    Dennis Prager, a West Coast talk-show host, reports the following: In his travels around the country he frequently addresses high school students. He often asks the following question: Assume you are standing by a river and a sudden swell washes a stranger, who means nothing to you at all, into the water. You are able to go after him but suddenly you see that your puppy, whom you love very much, has also been swept away. Whom would you save?

    Approximately half the students say that, owing nothing to the stranger, they would save the puppy.

    Prager then asks those students who claimed that they would save the stranger, what they thought of their classmates who favored the puppy?

    Most students have no criticism to offer. Everyone has to make the decision for himself. They personally favor the human, but if someone else favors the puppy that is their absolute right.

5. Midrash Eichah 2:48. If someone were to tell you that that Wisdom can be found within the nations, you would do well to believe him. But if he were to say that Torah can be found there, do not believe him.

6. The concept of a firm, and in many ways unyielding, hierarchical system is deeply embedded in the halachic system. We need only think of the ten levels of sanctity adumbrated in Mishna Keilim 1:6 and onwards; the various levels of ritual defilement described in the earlier mishnayos there; the division of our people into Kohanim, Levi'im and Yisraelim with the attendant halachos of preferment for the earlier two levels; the obligations of showing respect towards parents, teachers and scholars and above all to the monarch; to realize just how significant an idea this is.

Our Rishonim trace the theory which energizes this system to the very dawn of creation. Each member of the plant and animal worlds was created למינו, according to its own kind. It is from this strict compartmentalization that the subsequent prohibitions against *Kilaim* [the "mixing" of the "kinds" through grafting, interbreeding and the like] grew out. Even nature itself was to be hierarchical, with strict boundaries, never to be crossed nor blurred, guaranteeing the integrity of each מין.

Ralbag explains the necessity for these strictly enforced divisions. Only in a world in which discrete compartments are the norm, in which each element knows and honors its place, in which lower is lower and higher is higher, will man be able to recognize the One Who is above all else. A world without divisions is ultimately a world without God.

7. See for example Kesubos 96a. All labors which a slave must perform for his master, a student must perform for his Rebbi...

The precise circumstances in which this halachah applies need not concern us here. The point is that the Torah demands a relationship between Rebbi and Talmid which sits strangely with us who have been raised within the thought world of modernity as perceived by Berger.

8. The penultimate blessing in the *amidah* starts with the word *modim* and is known by that name. The halachah provides that we have to bow down [deeply enough so that the vertebrae in the spine become "separate"] at the beginning and the end of that *berachah*. See further below.

9. This assumption is probably based on the fact that it explains the punishment meted out to the snake: "You shall crawl on your stomach." The קומה זקופה, the erect stance which had been the mark of its grandeur, was to be denied it, and it would spend its life in abject groveling.

10. The word מודים derives from the root ידה which has a number of different meanings. It is used to denote: to cast down; to admit; to thank and to prostrate oneself. The common thread of a demonstrated submission is clear.

11. In the essay, *Taking Galuth Seriously,* we note this answer from Rav Hutner in passing. We discuss there the very real danger that such an attitude may breed an ugly arrogance against which we have to guard most assiduously. That essay should be read in conjunction with our thoughts here.

12. There should be no need to stress that I am not opposed to the constitutional rights which we all enjoy under the Fourteenth Amendment. These rights have been and continue to be a blessing to all of us and deserve our strongest support. Thank God that we live under a system which forbids discrimination on the basis of race or religion. [This said, we should note that some of the "discriminations" which are currently being jimmied into the category of those which the clause outlaws are, to say the least, outlandish, short-sighted and ultimately destructive to the society envisioned by the Founding Fathers].

The point I am making is that while the rights in themselves are an unmitigated blessing, the theoretical constructs upon which they are built are to some extent problematic from a Jewish point of view. Swallowed uncritically, they can undermine some very basic Jewish concepts. See further in the note below.

Flashing amber lights are a wonderful invention.

13. In the previous note, we made the point that while we enthusiastically treasure and support our Fourteenth Amendment rights, we have some problems with the theoretical constructs which undergird them.

The truth is that in these constructs too, there is much that we can admire and which resonates with our sense of the infinity of human worth. Still, it is our contention that we must not let our general approbation rob us of our critical faculties. כבדהו וחשדהו, "Respect him, but do not be gullible" our Sages warn us in a different context, and we need to apply this principle when we think about human dignity. For it is the innate dignity of every human being of which we speak.

In a seminal essay entitled *On the Obsolescence of the Concept of Honor*, Peter Berger whom we have already quoted within, makes the point that the idea of honor which played a significant role in the pre-modern ages, has fallen upon hard times. It has been supplanted by the concept of dignity. His definition of the two qualities reads as follows: The concept of honor implies that identity is essentially, or at least importantly, linked to institutional roles. The modern concept of dignity, by contrast, implies that identity is essentially independent of institutional roles.

A little earlier he writes: Dignity, as against honor, always relates to the intrinsic humanity divested of all socially imposed roles or norms. It pertains to the self as such, to the individual regardless of his position in society.

We can heartily endorse Berger's definition of dignity, although we would call it by a different name. It is the צלם אלהים, the Godly image with which every human being is endowed. [The disagreement among certain authorities whether this צלם אלהים can be, or perhaps was, forfeited by any particular people need not detain us here.]

Where the Torah differs from him, and where, if our thesis in this essay is correct, we need to concentrate the heavy artillery of our *chinuch* enterprise, is about the obsolescence of honor. While the Torah forcefully asserts the innate dignity of Everyman, it nevertheless vigorously affirms institution-based honor as well. See above in Note 6.

It is within the ambit of the "honor" mode that the drama of אשר בחר בנו is played out.

14. I make this statement in full awareness of the well known idea expressed by HaRav Moshe Feinstein זצ"ל that it was just this sentiment which drove many of the so-called lost generation away from their Judaism. Of course I do not mean that keeping the Torah in America is hard. Thank God we live under what Rav Feinstein himself termed a מלכות של חסד, and there are absolutely no obstacles placed before the most meticulous exercise of all our religious needs and predilections. All Jews should have had it so good!

I **do** mean something quite different. It is extremely difficult to keep one's ideas correct under the constant onslaught of seemingly benign concepts which are intuitively accepted and, in many ways rightfully, venerated by "everyone" with whom one comes into contact.

If you doubt what I say, test your reaction to the word "correct" which I used in the previous paragraph in the phrase, "...to keep one's ideas correct". Think what a rough time this simple and useful little adjective has had since "politically correct" [p.c. for the up-to-date and sufficiently sophisticated initiates] has entered the ranks of attitudinal bugaboos. To be perfectly honest, I used the term in the hope that it would raise some hackles. But, surprise surprise, even I, as I was writing it, felt a little uncomfortable at my reactionary certitudes.

Language is a powerful lobbyist. There is something to be said for our Chassidishe Yidden who teach their children to speak only Yiddish!

15. Introduction to VaYishlach. This assertion is based on two fundamental assumptions: The first, that מעשה אבות סימן לבנים, that all the experiences of the patriarchs "hint" at what would later happen to their children; and the second, that our present exile is the גלות אדום predicted in Daniel, that is that the defining character of all the nations among whom we are today dispersed is somehow to be traced to Yaakov's brother, Eisav. Both these assumptions are given wide ranging treatment in the literature, but the details of these very basic concepts need not detain us here.

16. We are not exaggerating. Herewith, a quote from Rabbi Ephraim Buchwald in TRADITION 32:4:

Our parents prayed for a melting pot, but instead we have gotten a meltdown! While, thank God, this time there are no storm troopers, no barbed wire, no barking dogs, no gas chambers, the net result is exactly the same -- no Jews. Prime Minister Netanyahu pointed out recently that since the end of 1945, the American Jewish community has in effect lost "six million" Jews. Since the end of World War II the general American population has more than doubled, but the American Jewish community, because of assimilation and low birth rate, has remained numerically the same.

Tragically, as American Jews were vowing "Never Again" ...one million American Jewish children were being raised as non-Jews (700,000 were raised as Christians and 300,000 without any religion whatsoever).

17. In the context of a short essay, it is not possible to piece all the various readings in the various Midrashim together. The interested reader is referred to the critical apparatus in Bober's Midrash Lekach Tov, vol 1, p.172. What I offer within is a paraphrase of what the record seems to yield.

18. In this reading, the frailty of the children is their inability to withstand the hell-fires of Gehinom in the event of their being unable to withstands the balndishments of עולם הזה.

19. It is very difficult to see how Rashi understands the phrase. He paraphrases: אתנהל נחת שלי [נחת] or the word for which it is a synonym, לאט, being treated as a direct object] which translates into something like, ...make my own unhurried way. But this takes אתנהלה as a normal active verb and ignores the *hispa'el* construction.

20. In the context of our essay on *chinuch* questions, we deal with children, not with the "flock" which also seems to have occupied Yaakov's mind at this moment.

It is with this issue in mind that we made use of Hirsch's rendering of עלות עלי in our translation, rather than translating in accordance with some of the other possibilities suggested by various commentators.

We have rendered Hirsch's German as: The sheep and cattle, still in the developing stage of their growth [= עלות], require my care [= עלי]. As Hirsch explains it, Yaakov's meaning was that his flocks were there neither for slaughter, in which case he could have killed them off, nor for sale, in which case he could have sold them. He was raising them to bear young ones and thereby to augment his flock. Under these circumstances, he needed to nurture them carefully. עלה carries the sense of growth and development and therefore also of healing as in phrase like רפאות תעלה in Jeremiah 30:12.

In the context of the Midrashic interpretation on which we have based our thinking in this exposition, the meaning would be very clear. It is only very, very recently that we, in our *galuth* state, have had to learn how to deal with wealth and comfort. Only *galuth* America has handed us the challenge of the possibility of unlimited material indulgence.

We are still very much in the process of learning how to handle it. We are doing some things correctly and many many things not so well. The last thing that we need now is to accept Eisav's offer of a formal share in עולם הזה.

21. There is, of course, also Succos when הדור plays a central role. But that is another story for another time.

PARENTS AND CHILDREN

1.   We have rendered נשר as eagle in accordance with common usage. However, Dr. Yehudah Feliks in his *The Animal World of the Bible* maintains that it is really the vulture. He believes that the bird is called נשר [from נשר, to fall out] because of the vulture's bald neck which looks as though the feathers had fallen out from there. He bases his opinion on Iyov 39:30, where the *nesher* is described as eating carrion, something which the eagle never does.

      If, indeed, the *nesher* is the vulture, the picture is particularly poignant.

      In western culture the vulture, as opposed to the eagle which is looked upon as a noble bird, is perceived in extremely negative terms. It is cruel, it is vindictive, it is the enemy. The name conjures up pictures of black and threatening ghouls drawing menacing circles in the sky, waiting, waiting for some poor creature to lose its battle with encroaching death. Then the plunge and the tearing and the pecking and the blood-soaked plumage. It is not a pretty picture.

      In scripture, things are quite different. The images which נשר is used to evoke speed, soaring heights, invulnerability, are all positive.

      Why the difference? Perhaps because we recall a different picture. We too see the vulture circling. But this time, above its nest, loving its young, exquisitely sensitive to their fears. God led us in the wilderness with caring and kindness, just as the *nesher* arouses its young (Deuterononmy 32:11). When waking the chicks to take food, the *nesher* does not crash into the nest without warning. It flaps around among the trees making all kinds of noise with its wings so that the youngsters should not be frightened (Rashi, there).

2.   One might of course argue that purely psychological needs have no standing in a court of law. Beis Din can grapple with the helplessness of old age more readily than with the wild longings which churn invisibly within. That, however, is questionable. Halachah is more broad-based than that. Thus for example, if a husband makes it impossible for his wife to enjoy the interactions which are normal among good neighbors by insisting that she neither lend nor borrow, or if he prevents her from going to weddings or to houses of mourning, she may demand a divorce. These are forms of mental abuse which she is not obliged to bear (Even haEzer 74).

      It ought not to matter that in those cases the husband wittingly creates these restrictions while in our case he is simply unable to have children.

3.   See Ha'amek Davar to Genesis 30:1.

4.   Except according to Menachem who offers this exact rendering.

5.   Hirsch, at Vayikra 20:20, offers the same interpretation. He points out that the base meaning of ערער is to stand alone and be unconnected to anything at all. This could describe an isolation expressed in either spatial or temporal terms. In Jeremiah, we have the spatial application, i.e. the tree stands absolutely alone. In Vayikra, where עריri is used to describe an aggravated

form of כרת, it is a temporal isolation. There will be no children to carry on his line as his time comes to an end.

6. It need hardly be stressed that whatever the Torah tells us about the Ovos is *sui generis,* and that it is not to be understood at the simple level of deceptively simple words.Their lives were made of such piety and saintliness as is beyond our ken. It is only because language is limited that words which are the same as those which would be appropriate in describing ours are used in describing their experiences. In every case, these words, when used in the context of the Bereishis narratives, hide depths which we cannot hope to plumb and undercurrents of meaning of which we can only guess.

Nevertheless, there are also the surface truths, and it is with these that the Rishonim whom we have quoted within seem to deal.

7. The healthy and entirely legitimate self -interest which governs our actions, is reflected in Rambam, Ishus 13:11. The issue is the husband's obligation to make sure that his wife has adequate clothing to wear when she visits family or when she goes out for some other appropriate reason. Rambam's wording is as follows:

...For every woman has the right to leave the house in order to visit family or to attend a house of mourning or of celebration, thus doing favors to her friends and family, so that [in her time of need] they will come to her.

Rambam's reasoning is realistic in the extreme. He might just as well have said that the woman would want to go to comfort the bereaved or to share the joy of the celebrants as an altruistic act of kindness. His knowledge of human nature seems to have guided his pen. Ultimately, it is our self-interest which guides us.

[I am indebted for this insight to my friend, the late R' Yehudah Naftali Mandelbaum ז"צל.]

8. See at Genesis 9:6: "He that sheds the blood of man, by man shall his blood be shed, for man was created in the image of God." The prohibition against murder is grounded in the Tzelem Elokim, the divine image, with which man is endowed.

For the meaning of this elusive term in this particular context, we go to Sefer HaIkarim. The passage is part of God's charge to Noach immediately following the flood. This cataclysmic event was to usher in profound changes in man's relationship to nature. His mastery over the animal world would henceforth be absolute. The eating of meat, which had previously been interdicted, would henceforth be permitted. But, Noach had to be warned that this broadening of rights should not be interpreted as a license to murder. Killing animals for food is one thing, but killing a human being is quite another.

It is the Tzelem Elokim which makes the difference. Sefer HaIkarim explains this as follows: In the animal world it is the species, not the individual, which is significant. To wipe out a species would be the moral equivalent of murder. To kill a single animal offends against nothing at all. Man is different. He is God-like because he is unique. He who sheds the blood of a man has destroyed an entire world.

9. We turn to *Berachos* 31b. In her prayer, Chanah calls God, צבאות 'ה, HaShem of the Hosts. Rabbi Elazar taught: This is the very first time that anyone called God by the name צבאות. Channah meant to imply the following: O God! From all the myriads of creatures that You created in Your world [מכל צבאי צבאות שבראת בעולמך] can You not spare me a single child?

Clearly our thesis is correct. Chanah longed for normalcy. In the teeming world of צבאות, where nature spreads life so abundantly, her infertility was a grim joke. Is it conceivable that God is so parsimonious that He begrudges her what He so freely grants the mosquito?

10. We point to Kiddushin 29b: [If there is only enough money for either] himself or his son to learn [Torah], his obligation takes precedence over that of his son. [Only] if his son has the greater energy and brilliance, should his son learn before him.

11. The absolute, self-sustaining, integrity of the individual is the subject of the mishnah in Sanhedrin 37a: When a human being casts coins from a single mold, each of the resulting coins is identical. But God cast every human being in the mold of Adam, and still no two people are absolutely alike. Because of this, each of us is obliged to declare: It is for my sake that the world was created.

12. Quite clearly, this does not mean that we ought to be selfish in dealing with our children or with anybody else. What it does mean is that our giving and caring do not derive from the centrality of our children to our lives, but from the fact that giving and caring are binding upon עבדי ה', people whose obligation it is to serve God.

CHILDREN--FOR DEPOSIT

1. It is instructive to examine the Hebrew word בן, son or child, in conjunction with אב, father.

The word אב is built from an א, which has the numerical value of 1, and a ב, which has the value 2. This construction is eminently logical in that, at the moment a man becomes a father, he enters into a relationship which defines him and his child as, respectively, source [א] and continuation [ב]. His personality changes, so to speak, from a 'one' to a 'first'. A second has attached itself to him.

What of the child? Is he defined only in his relationship to his father, or does our Hebrew language point to him as a discrete entity?

The combination of the ב with the נ in בן is significant.

How so? נ, so Maharal teaches, is the letter denoting lonesomeness. This because נ [and ה], the fives, can find no partners. One can always pair with 9, 2 with 8, 3 with 7, 4 with 6. It is only the fives which have no one at all, and must depend upon their own resources.

From here on, it is not difficult to understand the word בן for son. He is the second [ב] in relation to his father, but he stands alone [נ]. His is a discrete personality. He is his father's son, but he is also his own person.

2.   The legal term describing an object deposited with another.

3.   The legal term for guardians.

4.   At this point we should submit the mishnah in Kiddushin 29a to some analysis.

The mishnah deals with two categories of obligations: מצות הבן על האב and מצות האב על הבן. As the gemara works it out, the first category deals with obligations which devolve upon the father towards his son. Examples are circumcision, teaching Torah and the like. The second has as its subject the son's obligations towards his parents, such as looking after their physical needs.

Both Yerushalmi and Tosefta use these phrases in just the opposite way. The first describes the son's obligations towards the father, the second, the father's duties to his son.

The difference between the two perceptions appears to be based on disparate usages of the term מצוה.

Throughout Scripture, the term is always used from the point of view of the one from whom the command emanates. מצות ה' (Leviticus 4:2 and elsewhere) are the actions demanded of us **by** God.

In later usage it came to describe the action from the point of view of the one called upon to perform the command: מצוה על כל העומדים שם לומר..., All those who are standing there are obliged to say.... (Yevamos 106b. There are, of course, many instances of this usage).

The understanding of Yerushalmi and Tosefta appears to accord with the latter usage. מצות הבן על האב is the מצוה, the obligation, which devolves upon the son.

However, Bavli seems to understand the word in accordance with its Biblical usage. Taken literally, the phrase would have to be translated, The son's "orders" to his father.

The implication would appear to be that the father's obligations derive from rights which the Torah grants the son.

We shall discuss this concept in the body of the essay.

5.   A case in point: Friends in Israel have told me that during the two minute period of silence which is observed on Yom HaZikaron, they try to keep their children off the street so that they need take no part in what is perceived as a usage which is alien to our traditions.

I asked them why they could not just tell the children that the people who observed these minutes of silence meant nothing bad, that they knew no better, and that their expression of sorrow for their loved ones could be treated with understanding without necessarily sharing in it. Why not tell the children to stand silently, say some Tehillim or review a mishnah, and by their respectful attitude generate warmth and love in place of suspicion and hatred.

They answered that absolute disparagement was the only weapon in their arsenal to protect their children from being dragged into gradual acceptance of the prevailing culture. Often a minority within a society which flaunts its values with pride and assurance, cannot protect its integrity by any other means.

6. Megillah 13a and Vayikra Rabba 1:3 assign different interpretations to these names. We discuss the matter at length in Section Two of the ArtScroll edition of I Chronicles vol.1, p.402.

The limited discussion which we offer here is sufficient for our present purpose.

7. We have talked of living responsibly. It can go further than that. By refusing to live up to the unique obligations which unique abilities foster, we may actually forfeit our lives.

Naboth [who was murdered by Ahab's queen, Jezebel] had a beautiful voice. He would often go up to Jerusalem to sing and the masses would flock to hear him. One day he decided not to go and it was on that occasion that Jezebel found the opportunity to have him killed. What caused his death? It was his refusal to honor God with the gift which He had bestowed upon him (Yalkut Shimoni).

Naboth's musical ability was more than simply important, it was the central reality of his being. We would do well to consider the implications of this story in the way we bring up our children. A talent unrecognized, unencouraged or even, on occasion, quashed, may absolutely undermine God's purpose. A sobering thought.

Of course, we must be wary of drawing unwarranted conclusions from this story. Both in the case of Chiah and in that of Naboth, the gift with which they had been endowed was a pleasant voice, something which, certainly in the context in which it appears, did not need extensive training or practice.

We would be wrong to conclude that someone who displays a strong affinity for playing the piano, would be justified in spending hours every day practicing his scales. The development of our children's talents is not something that takes place in a vacuum. Clearly, conflicting needs must be weighed and priorities assigned.

8. Gra's use of the concept of mazal is based on Shabbos 156a. There, the gemara asserts that the particular constellation under which a person is born will influence his nature.Thus someone born under מאדים, the blood-red Mars, will have a tendency to shed blood. Education cannot change this. It can, however, direct him from being a murderer [bad], to being a butcher [neutral] or a surgeon or mohel [good].

This is the paradigm for Gra's assertions.

9.   Stories about the seeming inconsistency with which the premier educator of
     our generation, R' Noson Tzvi Finkel, the Alter of Slobodka, treated his
     students, are legion. In fact, of course, he customized his treatment of each
     individual to his true needs.
         Herewith is a sample:
         At one time, there were two students studying in the Yeshiva, one of
     whom was a studious and serious young man clearly bent upon improving
     himself. The other fooled around and showed little interest in either his
     studies or in spiritual growth of any kind.
         The Alter, to the extreme discomfiture of the former, ignored him
     completely but lavished much attention upon the other.
         One day, the first young man was sitting shivah and the Alter came to
     visit. The mourner was unable to contain his bitterness. Did tragedy have to
     strike before the Alter took any notice of him? Why did his friend merit so
     much interest and he none at all?
         The Alter explained: You know yourself to be performing extremely well
     in every area. When you wish to talk to me it is so that I might compliment
     you upon your sterling accomplishments. I see no purpose to this and, indeed,
     pandering to your conceit could well be harmful to your development.
         Your friend knows that he will hear no praise from me. If, nevertheless
     he craves my company it is because he feels the need of an anchorage so that
     he will not drift too far. This I am happy to give him (From HaMe'oros
     HaGedolim by R' Ephraim Zeitchik).
         The story certainly demonstrates that different people have different
     needs. However, as practical guidance for our own dealings with children and
     students it has its limitations. Its provenance is from a period very unlike our
     own. The toughness which the Alter displayed in ignoring the pious young
     man might well be misplaced in our own softer and more flabby society. My
     intuition tells me that today's educators might feel that even this young man
     deserved to be encouraged in his endeavours. Even if we were to recognize
     a degree of self-indulgence in his desire for notice, we would, I think, be more
     prone to excuse it.
10. We base our interpretation of the mitzvah of Tzitzis on Menachos 44a. There
     we are told of a man who, after vast expenditure of time, effort and expense,
     was finally in the presence of a harlot after whom he had lusted for a long
     time. As he was about to approach her, his four Tzitzioth came and slapped
     him across the face. Immediately he desisted.
         This story will resonate with each of us in accordance with our various
     and varying perceptions of what this wonderful mitzvah has to say to us. It
     lies in the nature of *Aggadah* that there is no single objective truth to which
     we must or indeed, can, aspire.
         Herewith are my own feelings. They developed out of my reading of
     Maharal in his Chidushei Aggadah on Menachos, and of Hirsch in both the
     Horeb and the Commentary on Chumash. It is not precisely what either of

them says, but both might agree that it contains a grain of the much larger and profound truths that these two seminal and creative thinkers tried, each in his own way, to share with us.

The following may be a legitimate part of what is certainly a much larger picture. The corners of the garment to which Tzitzis are attached seem to define its limits absolutely. They are clear boundaries beyond which, one would suppose, one cannot go. The Tzizios, placed upon those same constricting corners but extending way beyond them, mock this assertion. They are visible sign-posts pointing to an invisible and therefore boundless world in which animal lusts dictated by heart and eyes need not control us, in which the mitzvos designed by God to sublimate our physicality whisper of a sanctity that, against all surface intuition, lies well within our grasp. There are no bounds to human striving. We can, simply by investing sufficient determination and energy, reach any goal.

Our hero had thought that he was totally in the grips of his lust. He might as well not try anymore to overcome it. His Tzitzios came and slapped him in the face, giving the lie to his sense of powerlessness. They lent him the courage to realize that there are really no limits at all to that which one can accomplish.

11. We all know that the *kanaim* among us tend to lash out at everything that does not, in the minutest detail, conform to their view of the proper and the appropriate; and that those who see sensitivity towards others' ideas as the highest human virtue, tend to whitewash even the most blatant and inexcusable deviations.

Those who can condemn vigorously and fight mightily against that which is truly intolerable, but act lovingly, from profound understanding, even towards those who disagree with them -- such people are few and far between.They are the heroes who control their own lives.

12. Following are some examples of heroic self control:

As Joseph's brothers were returning from their first encounter with the Egyptian viceroy, one of them opened his sack and found his money lying there.

The brothers were thrown into turmoil (Genesis 42:27-28). What could possibly be the explanation?

They came home (v. 29) and told Jacob all that had occured (vs. 30-34). Afterwards, they opened their own sacks and, to their consternation, found that their money, also, had been returned (v. 35).

Apparently, then, it did not ocur to even one of the brothers to open his own sack while still on the road.

One does what has to be done when it has to be done, no more or no less. Opening the sacks could wait until they got home.

Or:

Before his death, Isaac wanted to bless his son Eisav. Clearly he considered him worthy. Rivka knew better, thwarted his plans and made sure that the blessing would go to Jacob.

What did Rivka know that Isaac did not?

Earlier, while she was still carrying the twins, she had been the recipient of a prophecy. She had learned from Shem and Ever that the older was to be subservient to the younger.

Why had she not, in all those years, told Isaac?

It is, because she told herself, 'Isaac is himself a prophet, greater even than those who passed on their knowledge to me. There is no need for me to tell him anything.' (Ramban, Genesis 27:4).

What need not be said, should not be said.

FIGHTING THE GOOD FIGHT

1. In our exposition of the metaphor, we have laid the stress on control and power advisedly. A careful reading of Psalm 127 seems to point to these qualities as the one upon which the singer wishes to focus.

    If HaShem will not build a house, then those will have labored for nothing who sank their energies into it.
    If HASHEM will not guard a city, then the watchman's constant vigil was in vain.
    Your efforts, those of you who rise at the first opportunity and stay up late, are for naught. It is so clear that He grants slumber to His beloved.
    The permanent possessions which HASHEM grants man are children. True reward is the fruit of the womb.
    As arrows in the warrior's hand... [see within.]

    There may be, of course, any number of ways in which the thought-world from the first to the second theme in the psalm may be bridged.

    It appears to me that we are confronted with a contrast between activities such as building a house and guarding a city, in which our actions are not of great significance for everything is ultimately in the hands of God, and the education of our children. Here, with the anticipation of God's help always in our hearts and our prayers, we are unequivocally in charge. He has placed the power in our hands. We can make a difference, we must exercise control.

2. We follow the psalmist in making no attempt to identify the enemy. It does not really matter who he is. The context makes clear that it could be any of the myriad forces that can and do conspire to undermine our confidence in the correctness of our path. A great variety of problems can and will face our children. Their success in dealing with them will be our vindication.

3.   This story is only one of several that describe events surrounding R' Eliezer's illness. We will offer a short survey of these vignettes as we hope to show that they all happened on one occasion. They help to establish the mood in which the maxims that we analyze were taught. This mood will be particularly significant as we discuss the second maxim, the one dealing with the education of children, which is the focus of our study.

Two of these stories appear in Sanhedrin 101a:

In the first, R' Eliezer's [unidentified] students enter and weep at his evident suffering. Only R' Akiva laughs. He is happy because these very agonies augur well for the great reward awaiting his Rebbi in the World to Come. R' Eliezer ignores the weepers but challenges R' Akiva. What had he done wrong to deserve this pain? R' Akiva answered that R' Eliezer himself had taught that even the most righteous must have some faults.

[Although in this story the visitors are identified only as students, it seems reasonable to assume that they are same men who are identified by name in the other stories. The presence of R' Akiva among them, seems to confirm this.]

In the second story, the visitors are identified as, R' Tarfon, R' Yehoshua, R' Elazar ben Azariah and R' Akiva. Once more, R' Akiva has his own approach to the occasion. While each of the other three sings their Rebbi's praises [Rebbi is greater than...], he concentrates on the matter at hand. חביבין יסורים, Suffering is precious!

Once more, R' Eliezer seems interested only in what R' Akiva has to say.

The most detailed account of R' Eliezer's death is given at Sanhedrin 68a. This time the visitors are R' Akiva and his colleagues. We paraphrase:

... They sat in front of him at a distance of four cubits.
He said to them, "Why have you come?"
They answered, "To learn Torah."
He asked them, "Why did you not come till now?"
They answered, "We did not have time."
He said, "It would surprise me if any of you die a normal death."
R' Akiva asked him, "What will be my fate?"
He answered, "Yours will be the worst."
He folded his two arms over his heart and said, "Woe to my arms which are like two closed Sifrei Torah. I have learned much Torah and I have taught much Torah. I have learned much Torah but have taken from my teachers less than the amount that a dog might lap up from the sea. I have taught much Torah and my students have taken from me only as much as a toothpick might extract from a tube.
There are areas in which I am an expert concerning which no one ever even asked me..."
After that the students asked R' Eliezer a question concerning the status of certain objects relative to the laws of cleanliness and uncleanli-

ness. He answered, "It is clean [טהור]." With the word טהור his soul left him.

The background to this story is the incident which is described in Bava Metzia 59b where, as a result of a disagreement which R' Eliezer had with his colleagues and of his refusal to retract in the face of their majority ruling, he was placed in cherem and had to spend the rest of his life in isolation away from the main center of Torah in Yavneh.

From the earlier part of the conversation, where R' Eliezer challenged his students to explain why they had not come till now and from their evasive answer, it is clear that all the stories -- the one quoted within and the two from Sanhedrin 101a, in addition to the one with which we are dealing -- all took place on the day of R' Eliezer's death. They had evidently never come before then. The various accounts simply deal with different aspects of that momentous occasion.

As we progress within and in subsequent endnotes, we will deal with the significance of the various conversations.

4.　The Hebrew is: מנעו בניכם מן ההגיון. The root, הגה, appears with two main meanings [see Aruch, under, הג]. One might be rendered, to think something through, and this is its sense in verses like Eicha 3:62.

But it also denotes to do something superficially. Thus Yerushalmi to Sanhedrin concerning the *sefarim chitzonim*, the books which were not included in the Biblical cannon: להגיון נתנו ליגיעה לא נתנו they may legitimately be given a cursory reading, but one should not labor over them.

R' Eliezer' s second maxim takes the word in this sense. Thus Rashi defines it as either the study of Nach, which can, although of course it need not, lend itself to surface reading, or as childish prattle. The Aruch suggests that it is the interpretation of a biblical verse according to its literal meaning.

In each case, the antidote is to make sure that the children keep company with the wise. From them they will learn the beauty and the rewards of intellectual rigor.

5.　The differing reactions to human frailties exhibited by Rabbi Shimon bar Yochai and his son Rabbi Eliezer when they came out of the cave a second time [Shabbos 33b] might perhaps be seen as bearing out this thesis. Old age seems more tolerant of human weakness than youth.

In the context of our discussion, it is of surpassing interest that only the first set of maxims found its way into Pirkei Avos. Obviously, the sayings which are recorded there are those which were most central to the lives of the Tana'im who taught them. It almost seems as though Rabbi Eliezer, in his personal life, identified more closely with the extreme formulations of his youth than with the more tempered expressions of his old age.

We should also note that the second set of maxims was addressed to Rabbi Eliezer's students. We cannot know whether he would not have made more stringent demands upon himself.

6. We will leave the third maxim in each set unexamined. A truly satisfying analysis would take us too far afield.

7. We believe that seriousness is the grand theme of R' Eliezer's living and of his dying. He cared passionately that every second be used to the utmost, that every experience be mined for content and edification. Nothing must be trivialized, nothing lost. Such a life is excruciatingly difficult to live; it is beyond the understanding of lesser men. Except for the great R' Akiva, nobody really understood him.

In a note above, we suggested that all the stories told of students visiting him while he was sick appear to have taken place on the the day of his death. There can be no other meaning to the bitter question which he asked of them as recorded at Sanhedrin 68a, "Why did you not come till now?"

What an occasion that must have been. The students enter and see their beloved Rebbi in dreadful pain; after the long period in which they had been forced to absent themselves because of the *cherem*. They burst into tears. R' Akiva laughs.

We have cited his explanation in the earlier note. It seems obvious that neither the reaction of the others, nor that of R' Akiva, is self-indulgent and instinctive without reference to the patient's need. We are dealing with our great Tana'im, not with children.

From the fact that R' Eliezer totally ignores the others but pounces upon R' Akiva's suggestion, that he might have done something wrong for which he deserved to suffer, we can deduce that only R' Akiva read his need correctly. A lesser man might have been moved by the palpable despair of his students. It would certainly bolster his sense of worth. This was not R' Eliezer's concern. He needed to know what he had done wrong, so that he would be able to make amends in these final moments of his life.

R' Akiva displayed the same sensitivity at another moment during that visit when each of the other three vied with one another in their appreciation of what R' Eliezer had done for them: Rebbi is greater than raindrops...than the sun... than parents...R' Akiva refuses to have any part of this. He has something more useful on his mind. He turns to his Rebbi, writhing in the agonies of his poor, wracked body, and tells him, "Suffering is precious!"

Once more R' Eliezer turns to R' Akiva, apparently ignoring the others. The atmosphere is as calm and unhurried as a long afternoon in the Bais HaMidrash. He is interested to know from where R' Akiva derives his daring insight. Perhaps he intuits, correctly as it turns out, that the source will, at the same time, reveal the sense in which suffering is beloved. R' Akiva provides the source. Suffering spells atonement.

If we could only have been present. If only we could have merited this demonstration of how to live -- and die -- seriously!

Why, as recorded at Sanhedrin 68a [the incident which we quoted in full in the earlier note] did R' Eliezer find it necessary to announce to his beloved students that none of them would die a natural death. Why did he not at least spare himself the dreadful task of telling his beloved Akiva that his would be the worst?

There is serious living at work here. Every moment left to him must be made to count. His two arms were like closed Sifrei Torah, that was history. Nothing would be able to undo the past. But he could still guide, could still instruct his students in the art of living seriously.

This is the background against which we must read the three maxims. These are the moments, these the attitudes which yielded them.

The most telling moment of all is the final one. Emotions have been roiled, tears have been shed, love has been expressed, guidance offered, fates discussed and now what?

And now back to what life, lived seriously, is all about. A question concerning the halachic status of certain utensils. This and only this, in the very final moments of this stupendous life, is what really counts.

The answer was, "Tahor!"

And his soul left him in Taharah.

8. We may be jumping a little ahead of ourselves here. It might be argued that the exhortation not to allow our children to lapse into superficiallity was meant only in the context of study and not, as we are taking it, in wider areas of life.

My intuition tells me that we are on sure ground. The formulation seems sufficiently general to bear up under our expansive interpretation.

TAKING RELATIONSHIPS SERIOUSLY

1. I suggest that the theoretical underpinnings for this assertion are as follows: The word כבוד, usually translated as *honor*, is often used as a synonym for נשמה, *soul*. This is so because, as Metzudos to Tehillim 30:13 points out, it is the נשמה which lends dignity to physical man.

   One who is מכבד את הבריות, who shows respect to others, demonstrates that he is conscious of the divine component, the soul, which animates his fellow man. Accordingly he is also מכובד, worthy of respect. He has testified that man, himself included, can rise above the physical.

2. The word for respect, כבוד is formed from the root, כבד, to be heavy.

3. Clearly, the Hebrew, גנב has a greater versatility than the English, to steal. Thus we have Bava Metzia 60a describing a merchant who places shoddy goods underneath some better stuff in order to deceive his customers is a גונב את העין, a robber or violator of the eye.

TAKING GALUTH SERIOUSLY

1. William Z. Low [Professor Ze'ev Lev, founder of Machon Lev in Jerusalem] in, Some Remarks on a Letter by Rabbi E. E. Dessler, printed in ENCOUN-TER ed. H. Chaim Schimmel and Aryeh Carmel, Feldheim Publishers.
2. Our thoughts in this passage are taken from *Der Neue Kusari*, by the late Dr. Isaac Breuer.
3. My apologies to such readers as may reside in other countries. I live in America and so its problems are more familiar to me. Much of what I write here would, I am sure, be applicable in most other countries also. I do think though that Eretz Yisrael should be excluded. The issues there seem to be for the most part very different from the ones we face here.
4. A profound insight is ascribed to the holy Kotzker Rebbe.

   The midrash tells that when God was about to create man, both Peace and Truth demurred. Truth maintained that man as an inveterate falsifier was not worth creating; Peace squirmed at the human propensity for quarrel and dissension. God responded by casting Truth down so that it could no longer object. Forthwith, He created man.

   How, the Kotzker asked, did this solve the problem? Even if Truth had been neutralized, there was still the objection of Peace to be considered.

   The answer is simple. Once you do not have to deal with truth, one can be at peace with anyone at all.
5. Kipling's call to "...fill each 'unforgiving minute' with sixty seconds worth of distance run" has always seemed to me to be a particularly inspired formulation of an exhortation not to waste time, a concept which he certainly did not invent. It is pithy and pocket sized and I have been able to slip it into my intellectual and emotional valise where other, longer and more profound *mussar schmuesen* seemed too bulky to take along.
6. We use the word weapon to describe music, advisedly.

   The Vilna Gaon in his commentary to Chronicles notes that the Hebrew term for music, נצוח [as in למנצח] is the same as the word meaning conquest.

   Through music, he asserts, we are able to conquer our יצר הרע.

TAKING MONEY SERIOUSLY

1. More precisely, *increase*. We have used the stronger, *bloat*, the better to catch the Torah's opprobrium.
2. The היתר עיסקא is an agreement between the two parties which technically changes their relationship from one of borrower and lender to a business partnership in which the prohibition against interest would not apply.
3. The explanation of the prohibition against lending for interest contained in this section, is taken from the writings of the late Dr. Isaac Breuer זצ"ל.

4. Chovos HaLevavos does not offer a source for these assertions.
5. We should make clear that we are not here talking from the formal, legal perspective. Obviously, as far as Choshen Mishpat is concerned, the money may be spent.
6. We quote from Midrash Tehillim 92:8.

A student of Rabbi Shimon bar Yochai went abroad and came back wealthy. His fellow students saw how much money he had made and felt bad that they had not had the same opportunity. Rabbi Shimon gathered them together and took them out to a valley. He called out: O valley, fill up with gold! Immediately the valley filled with gold. He told his students to take whatever they pleased. However, he warned them that what they took would be deducted from their portion in the World-to-Come.

Clearly it was Rabbi Shimon's purpose to deflect his students' desire to go abroad. He did this by miraculously providing them with whatever they wanted, closer to home. However, he warned them that if they took it they would diminish or deplete their portion in the next world.

Now he would obviously have defeated his purpose if money earned licitly would not be weighted by this disadvantage. This confirms our thesis that not all money which is legally ours may be assumed to have been earmarked to our use.

TAKING TIME SERIOUSLY

1. The mishnah immediately following the one quoted within, reads as follows:

הוא היה אומר:

1. לא עליך המלאכה לגמור ולא אתה בן חורין לבטל ממנה.
2. אם למדת תורה הרבה נותנים לך שכר הרבה.
3. ונאמן הוא בעל מלאכתך שישלם לך שכר פעולתך.
4. ודע שמתן שכרן של צדיקים לעתיד לבוא.

He taught further:
1. It is not your task to finish the job;
but you are not free to escape the responsibility.
2. If you have learned much Torah,
you will be given great reward.
3. Your employer can be trusted to give you
the wages for that which you have done.
4. And know that the Tzadikim's reward lies in the future.

The expression, אם למדת תורה הרבה, recalls the והמלאכה מרובה of the previous mishnah, the one that we are discussing within. Accordingly, the meaning of the second mishnah would seem to follow from the first. Rabbi Tarfon had taught, if we understood him correctly, that any proposition ought to receive ultimate validation only after it could be shown to be consistent with all areas of the Torah. The mastery of that vast corpus might well be beyond the ability of many. Those falling short would need assurance that not everything can be demanded from everyone. Even an unfinished job is not without value. Our shortcomings do not relieve us from the task of trying.

The second statement would then seek to encourage compliance with the ideal. אם למדת תורה הרבה.... If you did take the trouble to follow through -- if you learned "much" Torah, נותנים לך שכר הרבה, you will be rewarded for your persistence.

What form of reward is meant here? It would be attractive to interpret this reward purely in terms of enhanced understanding. For the true scholar there could be no greater joy. But our sense of aesthetics ought not to influence our reading of the text. נותנים לך, you will be given, implies something other than the joy of satisfying intellectual insight. Thus we must assume that reference is to an actual reward that will be awarded in recognition of tireless effort earnestly applied. However, the והשכר הרבה of the previous mishnah may well have the joy of broad-gauged command of the material in mind. This would avoid any problem with a troublesome redundancy.

Our assertion that an outside reward is contemplated here, is reinforced by the next phrase: ונאמן בעל מלאכתך לשלם לך שכר פעולתך. Your employer can be trusted to give you the wages for what you have done.

It is an action that is being rewarded by the Employer for whom it was performed. What action can be meant? No doubt, it is the fierce application to unremitting study that is required in R' Tarfon's demanding system. That application is considered to be, as the next phrase makes clear, an act of righteousness.

The scholar, whom Rabbi Tarfon typifies and extols here, is a hero who can be rewarded adequately only in the World-to-Come.

2.   We have rendered this phrase ...*though* there is much to be gained. This, because if the vav of והשכר would be a simple *and*, we would have expected a different sequence in the mishnah's statements. *The owner is insistent,* should have followed *The workers are lazy* [to which it stands in natural opposition] and only then should the fact that a great reward can be anticipated be given. As it stands, there is clearly the wish to establish a dichotomy, laziness as opposed to gain.

3.   These words are important. Obviously, no more is demanded of us than we are able to deliver. The tyro is clearly not expected to be as creative as the seasoned scholar. His involvement in the intricacies of the gemara must, at that stage of his training, remain relatively superficial.

4.   This passage should not be construed as a criticism of *beki'us* learning. There is certainly a very important place for that in any program of Torah study. But that too needs to be done with verve and energy if it is to be reckoned as an appropriate use of available time. Just *davening* through the words will not make the grade.

TAKING WORK AND PLAY SERIOUSLY

1. See Berachos 58a: If one sees a great crowd of Jews [Rashi: Six hundred thousand], one should recite the following blessing: Blessed be He Who is privy to secrets [Rashi: The inner lives of all these people]. For their respective natures differ from each other as much as their respective faces.

2. Our understanding of צלם, derives from Sefer Halkarim's interpretation of Bereishis 9:6: שופך דם האדם באדם דמו ישפך כי בצלם אלהים עשה את האדם. Murder, in contrast to the killing of animals, is disallowed because man was created בצלם. How is this reasoning to be understood?

   Ikarim explains: In contrast to animals whose value lies only in the species, man is singular [בצלם] just as God Himself is singular. Kill a man and you have killed an entire world.

3. There are other instances in which the needs of the community, even when there is no question of physical danger, preempt individual rights.

   An example is the halachah of נקיטת השוק, the "holding" of the market. This halachah states that we "hold the market" for a Talmid Chacham. Nobody is permitted to sell his produce until the Talmid Chacham has sold his (Bava Basra 22a).

   As explained by the commentators, this privilege is granted to the Talmidei Chachamim either as a mark of respect for their learning, or in order that their studies might be disrupted as little as possible.

   Either way, these considerations seem to run roughshod over the perfectly legitimate needs of the other farmers. They may have many important affairs that require their attention, but these seem to matter not at all. The community's need to encourage כבוד התורה, or to make sure that its scholars have as much time as possible to pursue their studies, is preemptive.

4. That the contemplation of beauty in nature can itself lead to a particularly deep and meaningful communion with God, seems amply attested by Tehilim 104. This is the magnificent paean which David sang to celebrate the splendor of the world as we experience it.

   Of particular interest to us is v. 26, where, in the middle of a lyric description of the mighty oceans, we read, שם עניות יהלכון לויתן זה יצרת לצחק בו, There ships make their way, [so too] the Leviathan that you created to provide pleasurable diversion.

   It has been suggested that the simple meaning of this verse is as follows:

   As the ships ply the vast and seemingly endless oceans, with sailors and passengers condemned for months on end to cramped quarters, unrelieved proximity to perhaps uncongenial company, an unvaried, tasteless diet and all the other discomforts of a long and dangerous journey, boredom and depression will surely set in.

   Suddenly, as if out of nowhere, a school of dolphins [לויתן, from מלוה, to accompany] appears. What endless joy they provide. Their friendliness is undemanding, their graceful cavorting a gift of love. Dreadful loneliness gives way to a sense of community. We are a part of something bigger than the prison formed by these dreary planks. Sometimes play can be very wonderful.

5. The interplay between these two elements plays a significant role in the thought of Rav Shlomo Wolbe in his Aley Schur.

6. In checking these sources, I noticed in Shemiras Shabos KeHilchoso that games of hide and go seek are permitted on Shabbos.

This reminded me of a story concerning a famous Chasidic master. His small son, a boy destined to become a great Rebbe, came running to him, crying. He and his friends had been playing a game of hide and go seek. It had been his turn to hide when his friends, tired of the game, simply went off to play at something else. He had been left in his hiding place, abandoned.

The father comforted the little boy. Is this not, he asked, exactly what happens to the Ribono shel Olam all the time? He also, so to speak, hides Himself from us, hoping that we will seek him out. We leave him in His hiding place and run off to pursue our other concerns, leaving Him abandoned.

This is something to think about.

7. What about competitiveness? Is it healthy or destructive? It seems to be pretty much taken for granted in our educational enterprises, whether in the form of mishnayos contests in the classroom or color war in the camp, that competition is healthy.

My sense is that it ought to be avoided. Educators tell me that competition is a valuable tool for encouraging children to greater effort. Hundreds of thousands of mishnayos would certainly have remained unlearned if the heroes of these competitions could not have expected the public adulation that is poured upon them as winners.

Perhaps this is true. But what about the child at the bottom of the list? And what about the victor? Perhaps it all comes out in the wash. Perhaps it does not. Somehow, even as I write this, I cannot shake my pity for the child who is always last. Particularly when, as is often the practice, charts are hung up on the wall giving the rankings in various competitive enterprises. Here he is daily and graphically brought up against his own inadequacies. I cannot imagine that this is a sound educational practice.

Rambam, in the fourth chapter of Hilchos Talmud Torah, counsels patience when pupils have difficulty in understanding the lesson. However: ...if the teacher can tell that their difficulties derive from insufficient care and effort, then his obligation is to show anger [לרגוז עליהם] and to shame them [להכלימם] verbally, in order to get them onto their toes [לחדדם]. Thus did the Sages teach [Kesubos 103b]: Cast bile among the students.[Rashi there writes that מרה, bile, is used as a synonym for fear: Your students should stand in awe before you].

It is apparent that shame, in certain circumstances, is a legitimate educational tool.

What is Rambam's source for this assertion? Gra to Yoreh Deah 146:11, feels that Rambam based himself solely on his own citation from Kesubos: Cast bile among the students. If so, this would not [specifically] yield a license to embarrass students. It could, after all, be argued that shaming cuts more deeply than, let us say, excessive corporal punishment [see Rambam, Talmud Torah 2:2: The teacher may hit [the students] to inspire fear ... but .... [only] with a small strap...]. This would absolutely delegitimize it as an acceptable educational tool. According to Gra, then, Rambam's assertion that shaming falls within the teacher's prerogatives would be his own interpretation of a source that is, at best, ambiguous.

HaRav Chaim Kanievsky, in his Kiryas Melech, suggests an alternative source for Rambam's ruling. This one seems to actually legitimize the use of disparaging remarks. Bava Kama 99b. reported an incident in which Shmuel's student, R' Chama bar Gurio, challenged a statement that his Rebbe had made on grounds that, in Shmuel's opinion were insufficiently thought out. He chastised him severely. לעכר מוחך, May your mind become murky!

But that gemara also seems suspect as a source for Rambam's ruling. There would seem to be a vast difference between a sharp word of reproof to a mature Talmid Chacham, who should have known better than to ask impetuously, and a yet unformed youngster whose self-esteem and mental health might well be shattered by being shamed.

The issue of the putative difference between children and adults is brought into sharp relief in another of Rambam's rulings. He writes: ...Therefore the teacher should never act light-headedly in his student's presence, should not laugh before them nor eat and drink with them. All this so that they should fear him and thus learn from him quickly.

As one source for this ruling, Gra adduces Shabbos [30b]: Any student who sits in his teacher's presence without [fear]...his lips should be burned...

Gra apparently read: כל תלמיד שיושב בפני רבו ואין שפתותיו נוטפות מר.... However, the reading in the standard Vilna editions of the Talmud, has, כל תלמיד חכם.... [See Dikdukei Sofrim, that the word, חכם, does not appear in all editions.] Gra [based on his reading] thus extends to younger students, a requirement which, according to our standard editions, applies only to the mature Talmid Chacham.

In summary, it may be stated that we are unaware of a really solid source to justify Rambam's ruling that a student who is insufficiently serious about his studies may be shamed in order to make him correct his ways.

We must conclude that to Rambam the matter was so obvious, that no specific source was required. If a Rebbe is urged to "...cast bile among his students," then shaming them is clearly an efficient way of doing so.

My sense therefore is, that Rambam's ruling may be culturally conditioned by the image which children have of themselves and their relationship to their teachers. In a society in which children were brought up not to question adults and lived with the idea that adults had the duty, and therefore the right, to discipline them by the harshest of methods, shaming may well have been the equivalent of the "small strap".

In more modern times, when for reasons which in many ways are beyond our control, children have no qualms about resenting and criticizing their teachers [and sometimes even their parents], it would seem that shaming them may well be counterproductive and constitute the halachic equivalent of the "scourge" or "stick" [שוט או מקל] which, as Rambam rules at 2:2, may not be used in corporal punishment. Such chastisement would constitute "a beating administered by an enemy" [מכת איוב] and "a beating administered by a cruel bully" [מכת אכזרי].

Simcha Asaf has published a three volume work, מקורות לתולדות החנוך בישראל. Here he has preserved a record of every available written record that is in any way connected with the educational enterprise of our people, from the period of the mishnah until modern times.

I checked the indexes for התחרות, competition, and found only one reference in the entire three-volume set. A short description follows: In the year תס"ח [1708] a קלויז [study hall] was founded and endowed by a wealthy citizen in Mannheim, Germany. The Klaus was active for close to two hundred and thirty years and was dissolved only in the wake of the Holocaust.

Detailed rules were laid down for all aspects of the student's lives. All was clearly spelled out: the subjects to be studied, the time that was to be devoted to them, the level of accomplishment and dedication that was to be demanded, and much much else.

Seating was to be determined exclusively by the degree of success that the student attained in his learning. The best student sat at the top, the second best next to him and so on down the line.

Now for the competition. Each student had the right, once a month, to protest his rank in the seating arrangement. He was permitted to challenge any student who sat ahead of him by claiming greater facility in reciting the gemara. Under carefully defined rules the two would be tested by the Rabbanim. If the upstart proved his point, he would be advanced in the seating and his hapless victim demoted. If the challenge proved to be frivolous, he was made to pay for his temerity. A fine would be levied against him.

Of course, the mere fact that such a system was once in place does not prove that it was good pedagogy. As reported in Assaf, the rules that governed the Klaus were worked out by the wealthy donor of the endowment, who had them checked out by, ...כמה לומדים מופלגים וחכמים גדולים.

We know that he was rich, but we do not know whether he was wise.

I suppose that most of us would not be in agreement with every one of the punishments that were imposed for infringement of the standards that were demanded in that Klaus. Typical among these was the provision that any student found pilfering even a penny from the home owner with whom he stayed, was to be paraded through the streets wearing a dunce cap!

This is not exactly what we would do.

Which leaves us with a valid question. Is competitiveness healthy or destructive? The jury is still out.

8.   I cannot improve on Akiva Tatz's masterful description of the insidiously attractive magnetism of the spurious world into which the excitement and stimulation of gaming inveigles us. I quote from <u>WORLDMASK</u>, p.122: "... at the heart of the experience of play lies the pleasure of an activity that leads nowhere; a pure game is played for no end outside of the game itself. And that is the secret of the pleasure inherent in a game: while I am engrossed in this game ... I am divorced from the world of my obligations; <u>I am in a state of being in which my goal lies within the activity itself</u> [my underline], I am not striving towards a point in the future, I am not looking beyond the present at all...Within a game is a zone of wonder, a zone isolated from the bonds and pressures of the reality of a life which is entirely obligation and work; ...it is precisely the nature of a game itself which intrinsically and deeply holds the domain of that escape."

It is beautifully put and provides a powerful frame to the argument cited within. The world of the computer game is not a world in which we would want to lose ourselves.

9.   I write these words during the week in which we read *Chayey Sarah* in Shul. Avraham's insistence that Yitzchak's wife must not be of Canaanite descent has strong bearing upon our thoughts in this essay.

Netziv in *Haamek Davar* wonders why it was necessary to send Eliezer so far away. Could Avraham's concerns not have been satisfied with one of the local women who were not indigenous to the land? Surely not everyone who lived there was of Canaanite stock. His answer ought to make us think.

He suggests that from Avraham's perspective, even a woman with impeccable non-Canaanite lineage would have been tainted simply by living among the degenerates. Canaanite culture and Canaanite corruption pervaded the land and poisoned whoever lived and functioned under their sway.

We in Galuth America have our work cut out for us if we are to maintain our religious and cultural integrity. It is so attractive to belong, so easy to be drawn into thought modes that propagate ideas and values which are inimical to our Yiddishkeit. The last thing we want to do is to expose our children to the crushing, albeit well intentioned, embrace of our hosts.

TAKING PRAYER SERIOUSLY

1.   This halachah is codified at Orach Chaim 90:9. It throws into question the propriety of the private *minyanim* which people often organize in order to

avoid the bother of walking to Shul. We will have more to say about these *minyanim* further along in this essay.

2.   Maharsha suggests as follows: Berachos 31a teaches that תפלה should be preceded by the recitation of psalms. Accordingly, since the synagogue is the place where these are normally said, it would be a natural location for the prayer which in the normal course of events would follow upon them.

    This explanation, though, would mean that Abba Binyamin's teaching can not stand on its own. We would need to know the other gemara before we can make sense of this one.

3.   There seems little doubt that we have here the key to the understanding of a difficult wording in the Rambam. In Hilchos Talmud Torah 3:13, he waxes lyrical in his praise of one who studies Torah during the night and never wastes the hours of darkness in sleep or gossip. In the course of his passionate espousal of this usage, he writes: אמרו חכמים, אין רנה של תורה אלא בלילה. He does not explain what this רנה של תורה is, nor why it can take place best at night.

    In the light of what we have learned within, the meaning seems clear. There are times in our learning when we need to feel in control, to have the sense that we are in command of the material which we have sought to master. But sometimes it is also necessary to permit ourselves to be overawed by the sheer vastness of what we need to know, the daunting depth and complexities of the issues at hand. That is the moment when we deal with the רנה של תורה, and it is specifically the night which is most hospitable to these feelings. Night is the time when we feel threatened and alone. It makes us face our shortcomings and inadequacies. It is then that we know ourselves to be on the outside, far removed from the King's embrace.

4.   I have tried to distill the essential idea of the Maharal as I understand it. Students of the Maharal will recognize how difficult it is ever to assert that he has been fully understood. I recognize that someone else reading the Nesivos Olam might interpret the words somewhat differently.

5.   It goes without saying -- but we all know that it needs to be said -- that the best *chinuch* is by personal example. It does not take more than a word or two spoken to our neighbors during davening, or a slovenly *brachah* mumbled at home without thought or feeling, to counteract all our well intentioned preachings.

THE SUM OF THE MATTER WHEN ALL HAS BEEN CONSIDERED

1.   We have chosen our title from Koheles 12:13, סוף דבר הכל נשמע. The translation is taken from Mesorah Publications' Stone Edition of the T'Nach.

2.   See the famous midrash to Koheles 6:7.

3.   Our comparison to life at the South Pole puts a modern spin on a well-known *mashal* by the Chafetz Chaim.

4.   I am describing the late great tzadik, R' Chatzkel Levenstein זצ"ל, Mashgiach of the Ponivez Yeshiva in Benei Berak.

5. It is customary in Lithuanian style Yeshivos to have a hortatory Mussar talk [a Schmuss] delivered before Maariv on Shabbos.
6. The great contemporary Mussar teacher, Rabbi Shlomo Wolbe, makes much of this Rabbeinu Yonah. Free choice is a מעלה, that is, a quality towards which one must aspire, not something that happens by itself. We may feel that we are choosing freely when in reality we are simply following habit or cultural norms and not at all exercising that greatest of human faculties -- to be unfettered in one's decisions.

מציבים אנו
בזה
מזכרת נצח

להאשה החשובה

רות רבקה לאה
בת
ר' אברהם ע"ה

In Memory of Our Beloved
Husband, Father and Teacher

Solomon Ralph Bijou

He Lit A Light In Our Hearts
Which Will Guide Us And Our
Children Throughout Our Lives

From His Wife, Children,
Grandchildren and
Great-Grandchildren

There Are Many People Who Owe Their
Lives To The Loving Concern Of

Ezra & Zekia Shasho
Of Blessed Memory

We Gratefully Recall Their Goodness
And The Wonderful Example
Which They Set.
They, As Also Their Beloved Daughter

Frieda Kredy
Of Blessed Memory

Will Forever Live On In Our Hearts

By Their Children, Grandchildren
and Family

*In Recognition of a
Generous Contribution
In Memory of*

Dr. Richard and Regina Weinberger

*Of Vienna, Austria
&
Baltimore, Maryland*

In Loving Memory
of

Esther Mezrahi

The Lady Who
Taught Us How To Love

By Her Grandchildren